An incredible story
about
the power of love

A kind woman here lies at rest,
The friend of so many,
The friend of truth,
The friend of age,
And guide of youth:
Few hearts were like hers,
With virtue warmed,
Few heads so informed;
If there's another world,
She lives in bliss;
If there is none,
She made the best of this.

"A remarkable, uplifting story from the man
called the Rembrandt of words." *Cue Magazine*

J. Wayne Frye

THE DAY VADA FRYE DIED

The Day Vada Frye Died

J. Wayne Frye

This book is written in Canadian English.

THE DAY VADA FRYE DIED

ABOUT THE AUTHOR

Wayne Frye's *Aaron Adams* mysteries, *Chablis Louise Chavez* thrillers, *Girl* books and *Lynton* adventures titillate the brains of those who enjoy tantalizing tales of mystery. His sports book, *How Hockey Saved a Jew from the Holocaust* is required reading in many schools. Growing up in the small USA town of Asheboro, North Carolina, he wrote his first novel at ███ waited over twenty years before finally submitting it to a publi███ s life, like the heroes he writes about, has been filled with grand adventure and excitement. He has been a college hockey coach, professor, and at one time, the youngest university president in the USA. Called a marketing genius by the *Los Angeles Times*, he has been a promotional consultant to hockey teams and motion picture companies, and he has been cited for his work with inner-city youth in Los Angeles. A proud Canadian, he lives with his wife, Lynton, in Ladysmith, British Columbia on beautiful Vancouver Island.

Some of the 59 Books by J. Wayne Frye

White Meteors and the Ghost of Sue Ann McGee
How Hockey Saved a Jew From the Holocaust
The Girl Who Stirred up the Whirlwind
The Girl Who Motivated Murder Most Foul
The Girl Who Said Goodbye for the Last Time
Something Evil in the Darkness at Hopkins House
Fall From Apocalypse
Armageddon Now
Worth Part 1: Like a Comet in the Midnight Sky
Worth Part 2: The Night of Thunder Road
Worth Part 3: Moonshine and Ghosts
When Jesus Came to Jersey as the Son of Thunder
When Jesus Came to Ladysmith to Battle the Angel of Death
When Jesus Came to Canada to Lead an Indigenous Rebellion
When Jesus Came to the Black Hills to do the Ghost Dance
Hockey Mania and the Mystery of Nancy Running Elk
Lynton Curls Her Hair
Lynton Walks on Water
Lynton and the Vampire at Tagaytay Manor
Lynton Buys a Cell-Phone and Hears the Voice of Doom
Lynton Viñas and Beowulf Perez in the Taal Inferno
Lynton and the Ghosts at the Mansion on Balete Drive
Lynton Viñas: Shadow in the Darkness
Lynton's South African Adventure
Lynton and the Stellenbosch Terror
Lynton and the Cape Town Ghost
Lynton, the Karoo Vampire and the Jewels of Omar Bin Abi
Lynton and the Haunting of the HMS Wind Dancer
Lynton and the Ladysmith Phantom
Lynton Viñas: Murder in Nanaimo - The Apparition of Dashiell Hammett
Chablis: Avenging Angel for the Forgotten in the City of Lost Hope
Chablis and the Terrorist Who Resurrected the Spirit of Che Guevara

J. Wayne Frye

THE DAY VADA FRYE DIED

TABLE OF CONTENTS

Prologue...........7
The Day My Grandmother Died
Chapter 1........13
At Those Pearly Gates
Chapter 2.......23
How Could I Survive Without Her
Chapter 3........33
My Grandmother's Anger
Chapter 4.........41
Get Out of Control
Chapter 5.......65
It is Better to be Miserable with Money
Than Without It
Chapter 6.......77
Angel of Death Who Had Come Knocking
Chapter 7........95
Defying Convention for the Sake of Love
Chapter 8.......125
It is Over - It is Done
Epilogue........145
The Day Vada Frye Died

THE DAY VADA FRYE DIED

To: Worth, Willa Mae and Lloyd Frye
Gone for so long now, but their star still burns
brightly in the hearts of those who loved them.

And as always to my beloved muse
Lynton Viñas Frye

Catalogue Number: 8341-945-910-2022
ISBN: 978-1-928183-59-4

Fireside Books
&
Peninsula Publishing

J. Wayne Frye

THE DAY VADA FRYE DIED

Prologue
The Day My Grandmother Died

The courage that my grandmother had
Went with her, and is with her still:
Rock from New Hope, North Carolina quarried;
Now stone in a graveyard hill.

The cheap brooch my grandmother wore,
She left behind for me to at lovingly stare;
I have no thing I treasure more:
It is something I love so fair.

Oh, if instead she'd left to me
The thing she took into the grave!
The courage like a rock, which she
Has no more need of, but I have.

J. Wayne Frye

THE DAY VADA FRYE DIED

She took one last deep breathe, and within her chest there came a gurgling sound, a sound that said to me – "It is over. It is done."

I had spent two weeks almost 24 hours a day by my grandmother's side as she lay in a coma in the hospital. Now, it was not a time to cry. It was a time to realize that death is nothing at all. It does not count. She only slipped away into oblivion, not to some magic kingdom up in the sky presided over by the omnipotent all-knowing being that has a cadre of wing flapping angel super-beings flittering about by his side ready to issue wings and a harp to my already angelic grandmother. She needed no angel wings, because she had already been an angel her whole life. When you die you die, and that is it for those of us who do not still grasp to fairy tales in adulthood, and at twenty-two I was a young adult when my grandmother died. Oh, but did she really die? She still remained in my heart. Nothing had changed in regards to my love for her. Everything would remain exactly as it was in my precious memories. I was I, and she was she, and the old life that we lived so fondly together was untouched, unchanged, because I would always carry those memories with me. As long as I lived she would live, and my love and reverence for her would be passed on to those I loved. Whatever we were to each other we were still. I would still speak of her in the easy way and with the tone of reverence I always did. I would wear no forced air of

THE DAY VADA FRYE DIED

solemnity or sorrow. I would still laugh as we always laughed at the little joys we shared. I would still cry at the pain we also shared. Her name would forever be the household word that it always was. It would be spoken without an effort, without the ghost of a shadow upon it. Life would mean all that it ever meant when it came to my love for her. It was the same as it ever was. There was absolute and unbroken continuity of that love. What was this death but a negligible accident that we will all eventually suffer? Why would she be out of mind, because she was out of sight? She would be placed in the ground, but her memories would not be buried with her. Memories of her would follow me until I took my last breath.

From an early age, we are taught to fear death, to fear that if we have not bowed in supplication before the throne of God, we will be forever cast into the bowels of the earth and endure the raging fires of hell for eternity. Teaching about hell is as important as teaching about heaven, because without one there is no need for the other. Fear is the factor which keeps us imprisoned to those who want to control our lives. My grandmother feared nothing, and she tried her best to teach me to never bow before the anarchy of those who want to manipulate and control our lives. She taught me that to fear death is to think one's self wise when one is not, to think one knows what one does not know. No one knows whether death may not be the greatest of all blessings, yet men fear it as if they knew that it is the greatest of evils. That fear is taught us from childhood, and my grandmother did everything she could to instil in me a lack of fear, a determination not be controlled and manipulated by those who want to make sure we do not think, because true thinkers are a threat to authority.

She had once told me in jest of something author, Mark Twain, once said: "Most people die at 25 but are not buried until they are 75." She was but 68 when she took her last breath, but I have thought often of that quote, because she had taught her children to truly live, to not be afraid to take risks, to believe in themselves and to never quiver before adversity or authority. She tried to teach her grandchildren the same, but I am afraid, in my case, I was far too often timid and an outright coward when I faced adversity. Even today, in times of turmoil I long to have her by my side for comfort.

Once when I asked her why she went to church on occasion, she laughed with a determined intent and said, "It's a form of insurance." How right she was. People go to church, in many cases, simply because they fear death and sitting in those pews gives them some insurance. The intensity of religion in the USA is why people do not die there. They "pass." Americans have immense fear of that word death, which is why they are taught through religion that you do not die. You simply pass from one life to another.

The power of religion in the USA is every bit as perverse as it is in Muslim countries, and school children are lied to about the history of the country all the time. They are taught that the country was founded by those seeking religious freedom, but the truth is they tolerated no divergence from "their" religion, which is why they burned those they accused of witchery at the stake, placed anyone who strayed from their interpretation of God's word in stocks to be publicly humiliated and shunned those who dared challenge their strict interpretation of God's word.

Although some sanity has staid the harsher elements of religion in America, today the Christian right is continually reasserting itself and aligning with a political party which is skilfully using them to maintain power and promote fascist elements in a nation that is actually fearful of freedom. Freedom is a word skilfully used by politicians, but it is a word that makes the power structure tremble, because those in power fear a thinking population will actually demand real freedom, which is why ignorance is not only an ally of religion, but is a way to keep people eternally trapped in a cycle of subservience to the privileged class, so that capitalism can grind down a large part of the population and relegate them to the true poverty of subservience.

THE DAY VADA FRYE DIED

Now, one may ask what this has to do with my grandmother, but it is highly germane to what she represented – a thinking person in a nation filled with non-thinkers. She refused to fall prey to those who want to exert maximum control through propaganda that promotes the lie that America is the freest and most prosperous nation on earth. My grandmother taught me to challenge authority and not to fall for the propaganda spewed from the government to keep the populace enslaved to a bankrupt idea of American superiority. She loved her country, but she could see through the veil of hypocrisy.

My depth of love for that woman is immeasurable, because she was a rebel and did not even know it. Neither did I know it until recent years when I looked back on her refusal to bow before ignorance and realized just how much I learned from her, and how my love for her has not waned in all these years.

I comprehended the day my grandmother died that love does not die with death. Love is a powerful liquid that pours out in a steady stream, and it seeps into others' lives as my grandmother's love seeped into so many lives. I am now an old man, and that love is with me as much now as it was the day my grandmother died.

J. Wayne Frye

THE DAY VADA FRYE DIED

Chapter 1
At Those Pearly Gates

*For the Angel of Death spread
its wings on the blast,
And breathed in the face
of the foe as he passed;
And the eyes of the sleepers
waxed deadly and chill,
And their hearts but once heaved,
and forever grew still!*

I lived my early life in the shadow of a great man – my father. Although he only went to the 7th grade, and at that he made two grades in one year, he was the smartest man I ever knew, and that intelligence was not only obvious to me, it was truly obvious to everyone in the small town where we lived. His reputation for being a jack of all trades and a shrewd businessman made townspeople view him in awe, as did I. Maybe that is why when it came time for college; I elected to go to school far from home to escape the giant shadow he cast. Ironically, I never escaped that shadow no matter how far I wandered from home, and even today, long after his death, I occasionally run into someone who has heard of him, even in other countries or from someone who has read about him in one of my three books about him. In fact, one of the books about him was in the top ten bestsellers for a short period in Australia, so he is even known down under.

This book concerns my grandmother and her influence on my life, but her story cannot be entirely independent from the story of my father, because he is a product of her and her husband, Dixon Frye, and the mixing of their genes produced an individual of remarkable talent named Worth Frye. Talent which I, unfortunately, did not inherit.

My grandfather was uneducated, going to the third grade as well as I can remember. However, education is not always an indication of how intelligent a person is. As I used to ask my professor colleagues at several universities where I was a teacher, administrator and hockey coach, who like me, had Ph.D.'s and were always complaining about uneducated people making as much or more than they were, can you rebuilt a carburetor? Can you overhaul an engine? Can you set the timing on a car? Can you replace a timing belt? Can you reline brakes?

They would still, in arrogance, reply, "I don't have to do that. I can hire a mechanic to do it?

I replied, "Of course you can hire someone, and their work in the garage is just as valuable as your work in the classroom. If your car is not running how are you going to get to work to pontificate and prance around the classroom displaying your intelligence? If things fall apart in civilization, I had rather have a person who can fix a car, hunt for food and do what you consider menial tasks than a person who can expound on Keynesian economic theories or Freud's theory of psychosexual development."

I learned to be sceptical of those who flaunt their education. My father and his brother Lloyd often referred to people who thought their education made them superior as "educated fools." I am afraid I fit into that "educated fool" category, because I frankly knew that I was not smart enough to survive without an education. Anyway, I watched how hard my father worked, often coming home in clothes filled with grease and grime, labouring 12 to 18 hours a day seven days a week and I simply did not want that kind of life, nor did I want to work that hard. However, I have always had respect for working people, the people who really make the world hum along efficiently for those of us who sit in our well-tailored suits or designer dresses behind elaborate desks and push pencils or pound on a computer keyboard. Without those working people, the world would actually grind to a halt.

I have always been appalled by the arrogance of the educated, the elite and the well-connected. It is important to not let arrogance go to your head and feelings of superiority deaden your heart. I always believed I was no better than anyone else; and likewise, that no one else was better than I was. I lived in Washington, D.C. in my youth and worked at the Pentagon during the Vietnam War. I had to deal with the arrogance of generals, politicians and well-placed officials on a daily basis. I even once went into President Nixon's office to deliver some top secret (eyes only) documents and was supposed, as required, to get Richard Nixon to personally sign for the documents. His chief-of-staff insisted he could sign, so I simply told him that "eyes only" means the person named on the transmittal form must sign. H.R. Haldeman, the Chief of Staff, was as arrogant a human being as I had ever encountered, but my father, my uncle, my aunt, my grandmother and grandfather had all taught me to never cower before anyone. I refused to allow him to sign for the documents. It was then that Haldeman called my boss, General William Westmoreland, who told him I was just following protocol for "eyes on documents." He stood by me, and refused to tell me to release the documents.

Another arrogant jerk, named President Richard Nixon came out of the Oval Office (I was not of worthy enough stature to be allowed into the inner sanctum of power that was reserved only for the elite) and without a word signed the paper, and I relinquished the documents to him. As he turned and started to leave, I said, "Thanks Dick."

Considered disrespectful, Haldeman ran to me and pointed toward the door as he said with the veins in his neck popping out, "Get out you goddamn disrespectful cretin."

As I left I said to him, "Sure, Bob."

In a democracy why are people expected to scrape and bow before anyone? Calling a man Mr. President is, in itself, no different than calling someone "your majesty." I refused then and now to bow before the authority of the exalted class. I show more respect to a homeless person huddled up in a doorway than to an arrogant jerk who thinks position makes him better than someone else. I learned that from my dear grandmother who never showed disrespect to anyone, but also never bowed before the privileged class.

Later, Haldeman wound up in jail over the Watergate scandal which brought Nixon down as well. Of course, Nixon was pardoned, because the elite never have to pay the piper. That is the reason Donald Trump will never be forced to pay for his numerous crimes. He, like all Presidents, and all but a few other politicians have complete impunity from prosecution along with all the rich.

One important thing I learned from my nearly three years in Washington, DC was that politicians, for the most part, know nearly nothing but think they know everything. I live by the creed of the Persian polymath, Al-Ghazzali: "Declare your jihad on twelve enemies you cannot see: egoism, arrogance, conceit, selfishness, greed, lust, intolerance, anger, lying, cheating, gossiping and slandering. If you can master and destroy them, then you will be ready to fight the enemy you can see." I must admit that in my old age I have conquered 11 of them, but that lust, even at an advanced age, is one I am still working on. Fortunately, I have a wife who says, without any rancour toward me, "When you stop looking at beautiful women, I'll throw the dirt over you, because you are already dead."

I learned from my grandmother to deplore arrogance, and the belief that no one should ever be exalted over anyone else has stayed with me my entire life. Of course that same attitude was illustrated by my father, probably as a result of what he was taught by his mother and father.

In regards to arrogance, there probably is no greater arrogance than that shown by the religious who do not want anyone to question the Bible or the Koran. On the other hand, I was always taught to ask "why?" More than once my propensity to ask "why" got me into hot water, especially at Sunday school. Anyone who "rocks the boat" and dares challenge authority is considered a threat to the social order.

I am not sure whether my grandmother was a believer or not, because we rarely discussed religion, but she did, on rare occasions, go to the church that was near her ancestral home in New Hope, North Carolina, which was about thirty minutes from where she lived in Asheboro, North Carolina. My grandfather, on the other hand, would sit in the car until the service was over. He always told me, "Them people ain't got nothing to say I want to hear."

Rocking the boat is something my grandmother often did at a time when a woman's place was assumed to be in the home, and she would not tolerate anyone abusing my rights when I would rock the boat. She once said to me, "Wayne, it is easier to nod your head and agree than to stand up for what you believe in."

Once, when I got into trouble in high school for refusing to recite the asinine pledge of allegiance, which the Supreme Court of the USA had long ago ruled could not be used to coerce children into recitation, she walked about three kilometres to the school when the principal had called me into his office and was going to expel me. She was inarticulate, and frankly illiterate, but she knew the law. She sat across from the principal who had his numerous diplomas hanging on the wall, probably to intimidate people. He said to her, "We cannot allow Wayne to defy the rules. We say the pledge of allegiance every morning and students are expected to participate in its recitation."

She, looking up at the diplomas hanging on the wall, said "I ain't educated like you, but me and my grandson has talked about this here pledge of allegiance, and I ain't got nothing agin' it, but he talked to me about what the Supreme Court said about it when the Jehovah Witnesses took it to court causin' they said it violated their rights, because they only pledged allegiance to God, not no country. So, you telling me that Jehovah Witnesses have to say the pledge in this here school?"

He took a deep breath and said, "No ma'am. They are excused, because of their religious beliefs."

She looked over at me almost with a smile pursing her lips, then back at the principal and said, "Well, maybe you should just consider this boy a Jehovah's Witness, then. I'd say you better let this boy go back to class."

"But he is not a Jehovah's witness. He is a Baptist" the principal said as he looked down at my records where, in those days, you were expected to put what religious denomination you were, and you could not put Atheist. I had put Southern Baptist.

THE DAY VADA FRYE DIED

Grandmother replied, "Just erase that and put Jehovah's Witness. He became one today."

The principal very reluctantly and with obvious anger, picked up a pen with some reluctance, and as he was changing my religious affiliation said, "You can go back to class, Wayne."

I placed my hand on my grandmother's shoulder when I got up. We said nothing to one another. We didn't have to. She was a mighty army of one who would go into battle on my side no matter how overwhelming the odds might be. From that day forward, for Pledge of Allegiance purposes, I was a Jehovah's Witness.

On that day, I realized that I must forever pay homage to a woman who was everything in my life. If I needed a friend, grandmother was willing to be my best friend ever. If I needed a shoulder to cry on, grandmother was there to listen. If I needed encouragement, she was there to give it to me. If I needed advice, she was there to give me the very best advice available. If I needed someone to understand any dire situation, grandmother was there to show support.

Even today, as an old man I reflect back on the golden times I spent with my grandmother and the wise advice she provided. The bond we shared was often one so profound that my own parents were jealous of it sometimes. She was, for a shy and awkward boy, someone who never wavered in her devotion to my welfare.

THE DAY VADA FRYE DIED

My father was an alcoholic, and because of that I would often seek solace with my grandmother, who would say, "I know he does wrong, but he is mine and I love him, regardless." Still, she stood by me, rather than him, no matter what, often defending me against him. For me, she was like having an army. This was my ultimate privilege: knowing that someone was always on my side, whatever the details or situation. Even when I was wrong, her calm, gentle love was the light in the dark tunnel of despair. She was both a sword and a shield against a far too often cruel world.

She would look at me, take me in her arms and console me with a love that I can still feel to this very day. There was so much comfort in her hugs, and I can even smell the scent of snuff on her breath. I actually wished I was a believer, because if I was, I know that when I crossed over into the next life there she would be waiting for me with open arms at those pearly gates.

J. Wayne Frye

Chapter 2
How Could I Survive Without Her

She taught me love and how to for justice fight.
She gave me strength; she gave me might.
A stronger person would be hard to find,
And in her heart she was always kind.
She fought for me in one way or another.
She was the person I called grandmother.

The youth of America are expected to be willing to lay down their lives in useless wars of conquest all across the globe in defence of freedom. How much freedom do you have if you can be allowed to die because you cannot afford life-saving medical care in an asinine for-profit healthcare system? How much freedom do you have when you sit at a table that is empty of nourishment, because capitalism dictates that he who cannot earn money cannot eat, even if you are a child? How much freedom do you have when government can deny a woman autonomy over her own body? How much freedom do you have when you can be denied the vote, because you have been convicted of a felony or are black or are Hispanic or cannot get to the polls because you are disabled?

These were questions my grandmother and I used to talk about, as she began, toward the end of her life to understand the fallacies of fake freedom in a nation that didn't really comprehend its meaning. She could not articulate her concerns very well, but one could sense her growing awareness that truth was being glossed over by those who were afraid of true freedom, afraid that the masses would revolt when they realized they were simply slaves in the great wheel of deception called capitalism. She was dead before Ronald Reagan became President, but she would have well understood the despicable nature of his mantra that *greed was an enviable trait.*

Somehow, American freedom is always under attack according to the government, usually by some Third World country that is only trying to throw off the yoke of colonialism or exploitation by corporations. This is the great lie of America, selling the idea that the USA is

J. Wayne Frye

the envy of the world for all its freedom. The world does not envy America. It fears the most war-like and arrogant nation in history. A nation that spends ten times more on the military than any other nation on earth while denying its citizens the social amenities that all the other First World countries enjoy.

I learned long ago that if you dared challenge authority, freedom is very quickly curtailed. My grandmother could not articulate that concept, but she certainly understood it. For example, when she saw the police in southern states attacking people of colour who were marching for their rights in the 1960's, despite being taught that segregation and denying black people their rights was permissible, she would say, "That ain't right, Wayne. The coloured folks is just wanting the same freedom we white folks have. What's wrong with that?"

I previously alluded to the pledge of allegiance, and the time my grandmother came to my defence when I refused to say it. Even in elementary school I remember those words from the pledge "with liberty and justice for all." I would often ask teachers why the pledge said that but there was not justice for people of colour. I mean I went to an all-white school, because segregation was the law in the south. At an early age, I could see the hypocrisy, but it became apparent that you did not question authority, and the authority which we all had to answer to insisted those words be uttered.

THE DAY VADA FRYE DIED

The pledge also says, "One nation under God," as if the USA is blessed by that all powerful deity. The word God was not in the original pledge. It was inserted in 1954 when politicians in Washington were worried about the atheistic Soviet Union during the Cold War. It was a way of reminding Americans that God was on their side.

It is so easy to brainwash people into believing things that are counter to their own self-interest. Like all other Americans, my grandmother and I had been brainwashed into believing that Godless, evil communism was out to take away all that illusionary freedom we had in the USA. How did the nation fight against this evil communism that wanted to take away our freedom? Answer – by actually curtailing our freedom through draconian laws that were used to imprison and/or ostracize anyone who embraced socialist ideas. In the 1950's, jails were filled with individuals from all walks of life who dared to question capitalism.

I was a very young child when I used to sit with my grandmother and watch the McCarthy Hearings in 1954. The early 50's were a time of great national paranoia and hysteria as the public had been inundated with fear of communism that was going to bury the exalted free enterprise system that made America so great. Senator Joseph McCarthy promoted the false idea that the U.S. government was filled with communists bent on destroying America.

THE DAY VADA FRYE DIED

This hysteria was all fabricated simply for political gain. I can remember my grandmother shouting at the television in anger that such a buffoon was given a forum to spread fear. I recall her saying, "Them Republicans think we are all stupid and will believe this nonsense. Why I fear my own government more than I fear them communists."

My favourite place to be as a child was on my grandmother's front porch on Friday and Saturdays, where I shared in the grand wisdom of my grandparents who helped me form a vision of the world in which I lived. Of course, that vision has grown and been refined over the years, as I reflect on their pontifications on that porch.

It was there as a five year old that I first learned to question religion, when I asked my grandfather about things that were in the Bible. His reply, "Son, I stopped believing in fairy tales when I was about your age." That statement from him would create an inquiring mind which was not appreciated by those expounding on religion.

A house where wisdom was lovingly dispensed.

THE DAY VADA FRYE DIED

My grandfather, who influenced much of my grandmother's thinking, was only around until I was 12 years old as he died when he was 57, but in my old age, I reflect back on his wisdom and realize that along with my grandmother he taught me to always be sceptical of what comes out of people's mouths and to think for myself, which is good advice in the age of instant internet communications and the Trump-loving MAGA crowd who gobble up and disseminate lies like vintage champaign poured into a golden cup. Although my grandmother was somewhat religious compared to my grandfather, I recall her agreeing with what he said often by merely nodding her head in a positive manner. She always had a positive nod when he said, "Son, when a man tells you he's a Christian, put your hand on your wallet."

Both of them had a healthy disdain for religion's hypocrisy. I certainly have embraced that disdain myself over the years, as I have seen how religion is used to spew hate and contempt rather than love and acceptance.

We are all products of our environment, and I am appreciative of my grandparents and parents who imbued me with a desire to think for myself rather than letting others think for me. Far too many parents and grandparents want to propagandize their children into thinking as they do. Although there were a few exceptions, generally I was encouraged to think for myself.

J. Wayne Frye

THE DAY VADA FRYE DIED

The 1960's and early 1970's was the era of the Vietnam War, and people my age had to face the draft, because, as was common in America, the middle class and poor were expected to fight for the freedom we had been propagandized into believing we had, but in reality did not. Of course, the children of the privileged class were given a pass. People like Donald Trump had doctors bribed to say they had bone spurs to keep them from serving. People like George Bush hid in the National Guard at a time when members of the guard were rarely deployed overseas. People like former Vice-President Dick Cheney, who never saw a war he didn't promote, had five deferments when he could have served but didn't. The list goes on and on with those who avoided service but had no trouble sending the poor and middle class off to die. This is the story of America and its hypocrisy. Even most of the signers of the American Declaration of Independence were slaveholders who dared to say, "All men are created equal;" consequently, hypocrisy was ingrained in the American psyche from the very beginning.

From my childhood on, fear of communism was promoted to keep Americans believing that the most serious threat to freedom was those awful godless communists in China and the Soviet Union (Russia). I like to think I was immune to swallowing all those lies, but I must admit that they did have an effect on me, unfortunately. When I graduated from college, I knew it was only a matter of time until I would be drafted to serve in the military. I had been able to avoid the draft for 3 ½ years because of college, but now I had to face the reality that I would probably be dispatched to Vietnam to fight those evil commies. When I discussed enlisting in order to be assured of a possible desk job, my father was appalled and said, "Don't worry about being drafted, I have a cabin where I take women with a member of the draft board, and he'll see your number does not come up."

I told my father, "Why would I let someone take my place, maybe die in my place."

My father, in his typically direct, no holes barred manner replied, "You think the sons of rich people are going to go to that goddamn Vietnam and die? You are a fool if you go into the army when I can keep you out."

Looking back on it, I realize now I was a fool for not listening to him, because the children of the privileged class did not serve. Yet, my time as an intelligence analyst actually opened my eyes as a result of a top secret crypto security clearance to the atrocities committed by the USA all over the world in the name of freedom, which was nothing more than a euphemism for corporate exploitation. Yet, since I spent most of my time in the service at the Pentagon, I was, through a close friendship with someone in classification and assignment, able to come to many of my numerous aunts rescues by getting my friend to place their sons in countries other than Vietnam. Most of them to this day do not even know that their dear mothers came to me pleading for help in making sure they did not serve in an illegal, immoral, useless war of conquest that eventually cost almost 60,000 Americans their lives in an exercise in futility that would eventually be lost. Additionally, my time in service allowed me to get my Masters and Ph.D. for free.

I enlisted in February, but because I wanted to be with my grandmother, who had a serious stroke, I was able to delay reporting until July 1. Thanks to the magnanimity of my father, who allowed me to adjust my work schedule with him, I was able to spend valuable time with my grandmother almost 24 hours a day.

I had also at this time become engaged to my future wife, whom I had to leave behind in Indiana, because I graduated from school in December and she still had 1½ years to finish her degree. Although I missed her, I spent a great deal of time with my grandmother, ironically teaching her to walk all over again, just as she had taught me to walk when I was a baby. She was making slow progress, and our time together was marked with great reminiscing about all the times we had shared. She was frightfully worried about me going into the army, but I kept reassuring her that I would be okay.

THE DAY VADA FRYE DIED

My grandmother was always a woman who put others needs before her own. On May 1, she encouraged me to visit my fiancé in Indiana where she was still in university, as she was sufficiently recovered from her stroke to look after herself and she had plenty of others who would look in on her. So, reluctantly I left for Indiana to visit my future wife on a Monday. No sooner had I arrived than my fiancé received a call in her dorm room that my grandmother had another stroke, was in a coma and she was not expected to live.

I hurried back home with great haste, fearful that she might come out of the coma and be expecting me to be there. Jamming through the valleys of Ohio and Kentucky and roaring through the mountains of Tennessee into the foothills of North Carolina, I kept thinking of all the times we had shared together, all the secrets I shared with her that she had kept from my parents, all the laughter we had enjoyed and all the times she had gently chastised me for transgressions while never wavering in her love. How could I survive without her?

J. Wayne Frye

Chapter 3
My Grandmother's Anger

My grandmother would lead me by the hand
Through that which I did not understand.
She was a tower of strength
Who would to protect me go any length.
How many times did she see me stumble?
Oh, but she would lift me from my tumble.

Usually, when I returned home from Indiana, I would always stop by my grandmother's before seeing my mother and father. Later in life, they would both admit that they were jealous that I would stop to see her first. Few people could comprehend the intense bond between my grandmother and me. This time, as I sailed by

THE DAY VADA FRYE DIED

her house without stopping, I sensed an emptiness inside, a deep feeling of sorrow that penetrated me like a dagger of lost hope.

The glass of hope was falling from the table
Set by a woman so loving,
And I had an emptiness growing
Like a lonely wind overhead.
Grey unrest was moving across my mind.
Boughs bent on trees straining against the sky.
Oh please, oh please, don't let this woman die.

There was agony building when the air
Moved toward my silent core of waiting.
With a single purpose time had traveled
In currents of that which I could not discern.
My heavy heart was burdened with pain.
Boughs bent on trees straining against the sky.
Oh please, oh please, don't let this woman die.

Between foreseeing and averting the inevitable
Lies all the mastery of life's elements,
Which clocks simply cannot in any way alter.
Time is numbered for each and everyone,
But I knew her survival was mine.
Boughs bent on trees straining against the sky.
Oh please, oh please, don't let this woman die.

There are shattered fragments of life,
A proof against the wind; the wind will rise,
We can only close the shutters.
While the sky goes dismally black,

THE DAY VADA FRYE DIED

And I set a match to candles sheathed in glass.
Boughs bent on trees straining against the sky.
Oh please, oh please, don't let this woman die.

I was roaring her way with the insistent whine
Of pain through the unsealed aperture.
I had no defence against the final season.
How could I survive in a world
Without her, without her?
Boughs bent on trees straining against the sky.
Oh please, oh please, don't let this woman die.

I went straight to the hospital. It was around 10:00 PM when I arrived and standing by my grandmother's bedside were her three children, Worth (my father), Lloyd and Willa Mae. I think they all assumed that I would react differently than I did. However, there was no need for tears or hysterics on my part. People generally cry when someone is dying, not as much for the dying person, as for themselves because they sincerely regret things they might have done or said. I had absolutely no regrets with the way I had treated my grandmother. I, of course, was fearful of losing her, but I understood that she knew I loved her above and beyond anyone else in the world. I took great comfort in that.

Willa Mae, in a voice laced with emotion said, "Wayne, I think she has been waiting for you before dying." How could I reply? I sensed it too, because our love was so strong that I figured she would indeed defy death to wait for me.

They all encouraged me to go home and get some rest after my 12 hour journey, but I told them that they needed rest more than I did, because I would carry on with the vigil and give them a call if anything happened.

It was May the 2nd, and that was the first night, as I sat by her bedside alone that I uttered words that would be my mantra for sixteen days: "Please grandmother don't leave me." I whispered it to her over and over, "Please grandmother don't leave me, please don't leave me."

I actually believed that our love for one another was so strong that she would defy death to stay with me. For days I waited for her to die, but my heart simply refused to accept that she might leave me. She couldn't leave me. She wouldn't leave me, because she knew how much I needed her.

I remembered when my grandfather had died, her personal agony, the long nights alone, and when she woke up, the years expecting to find him there, and only slowly growing accustomed to the fact that a part of her life would always be empty. I remembered the moments when she would find something funny and turned to share her joy with him, only to be shocked anew that he was not there. The worst moments were, when, sitting at the breakfast table, she would realize that she had forgotten the precise blue of his eyes or the depth of his laugh; that, like the sound of soft violin music, had faded into the distance where memories are silent. I asked myself if I would feel the same when she was gone.

From my sadness, as I listened to her laboured breathing, a feeling of great gratitude emerged in the dim lit hospital room. I felt honoured to have known her and blessed to have been so deeply loved by such a special person. I looked out the window into the darkness and realized that was where she was headed - to the darkness of eternity. I realized that my time on this earth was limited and that I should seize the opportunity I had to forgive, share, explore, and above all else, to love. I could think of no greater way to honour my grandmother than trying to treat people as she had treated them.

Despite believing that death, like fiction, was brutal in its symmetry, I refused to give up hope, because I could not let go of the belief that for me she would cheat death, scorn the grim reaper, spit in the eye of the angel of death. Her story of life was my story of life, because without her I would have no life. In my reeling mind I saw two miniscule white dots on a vast canvas, separated by a sea of intense blackness. She and I were the two white dots floating in all that darkness. We were separated by only a small distance, trying to merge so that we could, with each other, defy death that had come to call her. The two of us together would not succumb to the darkness. Surely our love could shine a light in the darkness.

I did not believe that there was some super being up in the sky to whom I could appeal, but despite that, I would often drop to my knees by her bed, reach up and hold her hand, sometimes gently kissing it, and I could still feel the warmth of her love offering solace to an aching heart.

There has never been nothing quite like the unnatural power that my grandmother's approaching death had on me. It was a pain that no medicine has ever been able to cure. It was a tumour that has been rooted in my bones now for all time, and it is a cancer of my soul that no surgery could cut out. It is an inescapable reality that has left a hole in my heart that can never be filled. The brightest days sometimes, despite some happiness, have often seemed dark when I think after all these years what I lost when my grandmother died. The warmest colors have often appeared cold. So powerful was the experience of losing someone I loved so much that it has dulled the senses often in a way that takes a person out of life itself, almost a death by proxy. I have endured, but not a day goes by without thoughts of my grandmother.

Perhaps it was fear which was the driving force as I pleaded with her not to leave me, fear that I would never find another confidant like her, fear that my life would forever be altered, fear that when she was gone all things soft and beautiful and bright would be buried with her.

I wished I had paid better attention to the moral clarity she imparted with so many stories that were intended to entertain but also to plant the seeds that elevate each individual to a higher plain of service for the betterment of mankind. Unfortunately, when we are young, we do not think of time as finite. I didn't fully appreciate the stories she told me, until I became an older adult, and by then I had to make do with snippets pasted together from fading memories with a rolling kaleidoscope projected on the back of my mind.

As I sat by her bedside, there were no tears. They were not needed, because I knew that she always carried within her heart the assurance of my love, a love that never wavered, even when she would chastise me for some transgression I had committed. I recalled, as I looked down at her frail body, the time I had caught the woods on fire in the vacant lot next to her house. My friend, Don Essick, and I went through a firebug stage, where we loved to build little fires. I had gotten over enthusiastic as the fire was roaring away and kept piling on more and more wood, even finding some cardboard from Don's garage to toss in the fire. He looked at me and said, "I think that may be enough Wayne. Anymore and the fire could get out of control.

THE DAY VADA FRYE DIED

I did not listen. I should have, because before long as I kept enthusiastically piling more wood and cardboard on the fire, it suddenly jumped into the trees above and started to spread rapidly. We desperately tried to put it out, because we knew we were in big trouble. It simply overwhelmed us to the point we had to alert my grandmother, who called the fire department.

The fire department put it out in a few minutes, but my grandmother's anger was not about to be put out so fast.

Chapter 4
Get Out of Control

The purpose of a storyteller
is not to tell you how to think,
but to give you questions to think upon.

Don and I bowed our heads in contriteness, but my grandmother was not going to just let things go with an "I'm sorry."

She looked at Don and asked him, "Why do we have fire?"

Don, without hesitation said, "To cook."

She then turned to me and asked, "And Wayne, what else to have fire for?"

Timidly, I replied, "Well, it can keep us warm when it is cold."

THE DAY VADA FRYE DIED

She, shaking her head affirmatively, said, "Yes, that is right, so fire is not always bad. I mean you boys made it bad today, but let me tell you a story about the value of fire, and you think about what I am trying to tell you, trying to make you understand."

The Fire Story (Rewritten in my words)

Way up north, close to Alaska, there is a place called, the Yukon. It was there that a lone man turned aside from the main Yukon trail. He climbed the high earth-bank where a little-traveled trail led east through the pine forest. It was a high bank, and he paused to breathe at the top. He excused the act to himself by looking at his watch. It was nine o'clock in the morning. There was no sun or promise of sun, although there was not a cloud in the sky. It was a clear day. However, there seemed to be an indescribable darkness over the face of things. That was because the sun was absent from the sky. This fact did not worry the man. He was not alarmed by the lack of sun. It had been days since he had seen the sun, because in the winter there was perpetual night in the Yukon. The man very wide and hidden under three feet of ice. On top of this ice were as many feet of snow. It was all pure white. North and south, as far as his eye could see it was unbroken white. The one thing that relieved the whiteness was a thin dark line that curved from the pine-covered island to the south. It curved into the north, where it disappeared behind another pine-covered island. This dark line was the trail—the main trail. It led south 800 kilometres to the Chilcoot Pass and salt water. It led north 150 kilometres to Dawson City, and still farther on to the north a thousand kilometres to Nulato, and finally to St. Michael, on the Bering Sea. But all this—the distant trail, no sun in the sky, the great cold, and the strangeness of it all—had no effect on the man. It was not because he was long familiar with it. He was a newcomer in the land, and this was his first winter. The trouble with him was that he was not able to imagine. He was quick and ready in the things of life, but only in the things, and not in their meanings. Fifty degrees below zero meant 80 degrees of frost. Such facts told him that it was cold and uncomfortable, and that was all. It did not lead him to consider his weaknesses as a creature affected by temperature. Nor did he think about man's general weakness, able to live only within narrow limits of heat and cold. From there, it did not lead him to thoughts of heaven and the meaning of a man's life. 50 degrees below zero meant a bite of frost that hurt and that must be guarded against by the use of mittens, ear coverings, warm moccasins, and thick socks. 50 degrees below zero was to him nothing more than 50 degrees below zero. That it should be more important than that was a thought that never entered his head. As he turned to go, he forced some water from his mouth as an experiment. There was a sudden noise that surprised him. He tried it again. And again, in the air, before they could fall to the snow, the drops of spit became ice that broke with a noise. He knew that at 50 below zero water from the mouth made a noise when it hit the snow. But this had done that in the air. Undoubtedly it was colder than 50 below. But exactly how much colder he did not know. But the temperature did not matter. He was headed for the old camp on Henderson Creek, where there was a settlement and there would be plenty of fires.

He had taken the long trail to look at the possibility of floating logs from the islands in the Yukon down the river when the ice melted. He would be in camp by six o'clock that evening. It might be a little after that, but the boys would be there, a fire would be burning, and a hot supper would be ready. As he thought of lunch, he pressed his hand against the package under his jacket. It was also under his shirt, wrapped in a handkerchief, and lying for warmth against the naked skin. Otherwise, the bread would freeze.

He smiled contentedly to himself as he thought of those pieces of bread, each of which enclosed a generous portion of cooked meat. He plunged among the big pine trees. The trail was not well marked there. Several feet of snow had fallen since he had passed the last sled. He was glad he was without a sled. Actually, he carried nothing but the lunch wrapped in the handkerchief. He was surprised, however, at the cold. It certainly was cold, he decided, as he rubbed his nose and face with his mittened hand. He had a good growth of hair on his face, but that did not protect his nose or the upper part of his face from the frosty air. Following at the man's heels was a big native dog. It was a wolf dog, grey-coated and not noticeably different from its brother, the wild wolf. The animal was worried by the great cold. It knew that this was no time for traveling. Its own feeling was closer to the truth than the man's judgment. In reality, it was not merely colder than 50 below zero; it was colder than 60 below, than 70 below. It was 75 below zero.

The dog did not know anything about temperatures. Possibly in its brain there was no understanding of a condition of very cold, such as was in the man's brain. But the animal sensed the danger. Its fear made it question eagerly every movement of the man as if expecting him to go into camp or to seek shelter somewhere and build a fire. The dog had learned about fire, and it wanted fire. Otherwise, it would dig itself into the snow and find shelter from the cold air.

The frozen moistness of its breathing had settled on its fur in a fine powder of frost. The hair on the man's face was similarly frosted, but more solidly. It took the form of ice and increased with every warm, moist breath from his mouth. He continued through the level forest for maybe an hour. Then he went down a bank to the frozen path of a small stream. This was Henderson Creek and he knew he was near from where the stream divided. He looked at his watch. It was ten o'clock. He was traveling at a pretty good rate. Thus, he figured that he would arrive where the stream divided at half-past twelve. He decided he would eat his lunch when he arrived there.

The dog followed again at his heels, with its tail hanging low, as the man started to walk along the frozen stream. The old sled trail could be seen, but the snow covered the marks of the last sleds. In a month no man had traveled up or down that silent creek. The man went steadily ahead. He was not much of a thinker. At that moment he had nothing to think about except that he would eat lunch at the stream's divide and that at six o'clock he would be in camp with the others.

There was nobody to talk to; and, had there been, speech would not have been possible because of the ice around his mouth. Once in a while the thought repeated itself that it was very cold and that he had never experienced such cold. As he walked along, he rubbed his face and nose with the back of his mittened hand. He did this without thinking, frequently changing hands. But, with all his rubbing, the instant he stopped, his face and nose became numb. His face would surely be frozen. He knew that and he was sorry that he had not worn the sort of nose guard needed in the intense cold. Such a guard passed across the nose and covered the entire face.

What was a little frost? A bit painful, that was all. It was never serious. Empty as the man's rambling thoughts, he was most observant. He noticed the changes in the creek, the curves and the bends. And always he noted where he placed his feet. Once, coming around a bend, he moved suddenly to the side, like a frightened horse. He curved away from the place where he had been walking and retraced his steps several feet along the trail. He knew the creek was frozen to the bottom. No creek could contain water in that winter. But he knew also that there were streams of water that came out from the hillsides and ran along under the snow and on top of the ice of the creek. He knew that even in the coldest weather these streams were never frozen, and he also knew their danger. They hid pools of water under the snow that might be three inches deep, or three feet. Sometimes a skin of ice half an inch thick covered them, and in turn was covered by the snow. Sometimes there was both water and thin ice, and when a man broke through he could get very wet. That was why he had jumped away so suddenly. He had felt the ice move under his feet. He had also heard the noise of the snow-covered ice skin breaking. And to get his feet wet in such a temperature meant trouble and danger. At the very least it meant delay, because he would be forced to stop and build a fire. Only under its protection could he bare his feet while he dried his socks and moccasins.

He stood and studied the creek bottom and its banks. He decided that the flowing stream of water came from the right side. He thought a while, rubbing his nose and face. Then he walked to the left. He stepped carefully and tested the ice at each step. Once away from the danger, he continued at his usual pace.

During the next two hours he came to several similar dangers. Usually the snow above the pools had a sunken appearance. However, once again he came near to falling through the ice. Once, sensing danger, he made the dog go ahead. The dog did not want to go. It hesitated until the man pushed it forward. Then it went quickly across the white, unbroken surface. Suddenly it fell through the ice, but climbed out on the other side, which was firm. It had wet its feet and legs. Almost immediately the water on them turned to ice. The dog made quick efforts to get the ice off its legs.

The man removed the mitten from his right hand and helped the dog tear out the pieces of ice. He did not bare his fingers more than a minute, and was surprised to find that they were numb. It certainly was cold. He pulled on the mitten quickly and beat the hand across his breast. At twelve o'clock the day was at its brightest. Yet he knew there would be no sun in the sky. At half-past twelve, on the minute, he arrived at the divide of the creek. He was pleased at his rate of speed. If he continued, he would certainly be at Henderson Creek Town by six o'clock that evening. He unbuttoned his jacket and shirt and pulled forth his lunch. The action took no more than a quarter of a minute, yet in that brief moment the numbness touched his bare fingers.

He did not put the mitten on, but instead, struck the fingers against his leg. Then he sat down on a snow-covered log to eat. The pain that followed the striking of his fingers against his leg ceased so quickly that he was frightened. He had not had time to take a bite of his lunch. He struck the fingers repeatedly and returned them to the mitten. Then he bared the other hand for the purpose of eating. He tried to take a mouthful, but the ice around his mouth prevented him. Then he knew what was wrong. He had forgotten to build a fire and warm himself. He laughed at his own foolishness. As he laughed, he noted the numbness in his bare fingers. Also, he noted that the feeling which had first come to his toes when he sat down was already passing away. He wondered whether the toes were warm or whether they were numb. He moved them inside the moccasins and decided that they were numb. He pulled the mitten on hurriedly and stood up. He was somewhat frightened. He stamped forcefully until the feeling returned to his feet. It certainly was cold he thought. That man from Sulphur Creek had spoken the truth when telling how cold it sometimes got in this country. And he had laughed at him at the time!

That showed one must not be too sure of things. There was no mistake about it, it was cold. He walked a few steps, stamping his feet and waving his arms, until reassured by the returning warmth. Then he took some matches and proceeded to make a fire. In the bushes, the high water had left a supply of sticks. From there he got wood for his fire. Working carefully from a small beginning, he soon had a roaring fire. Bending over the fire, he first melted the ice from his face. With the protection of the fire's warmth he ate his lunch.

For the moment, the cold had been forced away. The dog took comfort in the fire, lying at full length close enough for warmth and far enough away to escape being burned. He pulled on his mittens, settled his cap firmly about his ears, and started along the creek trail toward the left. The dog was sorry to leave and looked back toward the fire. This man did not know cold. Possibly none of his ancestors had known cold, real cold. But the dog knew and all of its family knew. And it knew that it was not good to walk outside in such fearful cold. It was the time to lie in a hole in the snow and to wait for this awful cold to stop. There was no real bond between the dog and the man. The one was the slave of the other. The dog made no effort to indicate its fears to the man. It was not concerned with the well-being of the man. It was for its own sake that it looked toward the fire. But the man whistled, and spoke to it with the sound of the whip in his voice. So, the dog started walking close to the man's heels and followed him along the trail.

There did not seem to be so many pools of water under the snow on the left side of Henderson Creek, and for half an hour the man saw no signs of any. Then it happened. At a place where there were no signs, the man broke through. It was not deep. He was wet to the knees before he got out of the water to the firm snow. He was angry and cursed his luck aloud. He had hoped to get into camp at six o'clock, and this would delay him an hour. Now he would have to build a fire and dry his moccasins and socks. This was most important at that low temperature. He knew that much. So he turned aside to the bank, which he climbed. On top, under several small pine trees, he found some firewood which had been carried there by the high water of the previous year. There were some sticks, but also larger branches, and some dry grasses. Just like you Wayne, he kept building the fire to a roaring blaze. He worked slowly and carefully. Gradually, as the flame grew stronger, he increased the size of the sticks with which he fed it. He sat in the snow, pulling the sticks from the bushes under the trees and feeding them directly to the flame. He knew he must not fail. When it is 75 below zero, a man must not fail in his first attempt to build a fire. Now, understand that this fire was for survival, but Wayne your fire was for fun. There is a big difference.

Already all feeling had gone from his feet. To build the fire he had been forced to remove his mittens, and the fingers had quickly become numb. The pace of his walking had kept his heart pushing the blood to all parts of his body. But the instant he stopped, the action of the heart slowed down. He now received the full force of the cold. The blood of his body drew back from it. The blood was alive, like the dog. Like the dog, it wanted to hide and seek cover, away from the fearful cold. As long as he had walked, the blood rose to the surface. But now it sank down into the lowest depths of his body. His feet and hands were the first to feel its absence. His wet feet froze first. His bare fingers were numb, although they had not yet begun to freeze. Nose and face were already freezing, while the skin of all his body became cold as it lost its blood. But he was safe. Toes and nose and face would be only touched by the frost, because the fire was beginning to burn with strength. He was feeding it with sticks the size of his finger. In another minute he would be able to feed it with larger branches. Then he could remove his wet moccasins and socks. While they dried, he could keep his naked feet warm by the fire. The fire was a roaring success. He was safe. Here he was alone; and he had managed to save himself thanks to the fire. Still it was surprising, the rapidity with which his face and nose were freezing. And he had not thought his fingers could lose their feeling in so short a time. Without feeling they were, because he found it very difficult to make them move together to grasp a stick. They seemed far from his body and from him. When he touched a stick, he had to look to see whether or not he was holding it. All of which mattered little. There was the fire, promising life with every dancing flame. He started to untie his moccasins. They were coated with ice. The thick socks were like iron almost to the knees. The moccasin's strings were like ropes of steel. For a moment he pulled them with his unfeeling fingers. Then, realizing the foolishness of it, he grasped his knife. But before he could cut the strings, it happened. It was his own fault, his mistake. He should not have built the fire under the pine tree. He should have built it in an open space. But it had been easier to pull the sticks from the bushes and drop them directly on the fire. Now the tree under which he had done this carried a weight of snow on its branches. No wind had been blowing for weeks and each branch was heavy with snow. Each time he pulled a stick he shook the tree slightly. There had been just enough movement to cause the awful thing to happen.

THE DAY VADA FRYE DIED

High up in the tree one branch dropped its load of snow. This fell on the branches beneath. This process continued, spreading through the whole tree. The snow fell without warning upon the man and the fire, and the fire was dead.

Where the fire had burned was a pile of fresh snow. The man was shocked. It was like hearing his own judgment of death. For a moment he sat and stared at the spot where the fire had been. Then he grew very calm. He realized that he must build the fire again, and this second time he must not fail. Even if he succeeded, he would be likely to lose some toes. His feet must be badly frozen by now, and there would be some time before the second fire was ready. Such were his thoughts, but he did not sit and think them. He was busy all the time they were passing through his mind. He made a new foundation for a fire, this time in the open space, where no tree would be above it. He realized like I hope Wayne does now that you never build a fire near a tree.

He gathered dry grasses and tiny sticks. He could not bring his fingers together to pull them out of the ground, but he was able to gather them by the handful. In this way he also got many pieces that were undesirable, but it was the best he could do. He worked carefully, even collecting an armful of the larger branches to be used later when the fire gathered strength. All that time the dog sat and watched

J. Wayne Frye

him. There was an anxious look in its eyes, because it depended upon him as the fire provider, and the fire was slow in coming.

When all was ready, the man reached in his pocket for matches. He knew they were there, but he could not feel it with his numb fingers. He tried again and again, but he could not grasp it. And all the time, in his mind, he knew that each instant his feet were freezing. This thought greatly alarmed him, but he fought against it and kept calm. He pulled on his mittens with his teeth, and began swinging his arms. Then he beat his hands with all his strength against his sides. He did this while he was sitting down. Then he stood up to do it. All the while the dog sat in the snow, its tail curled warmly over its feet and its sharp wolf ears bent forward as it looked at the man. And the man, as he waved his arms and hands, looked with longing at the creature that was warm and secure in the covering provided by nature. After a time, he began to notice some feeling in his beaten fingers. The feeling grew stronger until it became very painful, but the man welcomed the pain. He pulled the mitten from his right hand and grasped the match from his pocket, but the awful cold had already driven the life out of his fingers. In his effort to separate one match from the others, the whole pack fell in the snow. He tried to pick one out of the snow, but failed. The dead fingers could neither touch nor hold.

THE DAY VADA FRYE DIED

Now he was very careful. He drove the thought of his freezing feet, and nose, and face, from his mind. He devoted his whole soul to picking up the matches. He followed the movement of his fingers with his eyes, using his sense of sight instead of that of touch. When he saw his fingers on each side of the pack, he closed them. That is, he willed to close them, because the fingers did not obey. He put the mitten on the right hand again, and beat it fiercely against his knee. Then, with both mittened hands, he lifted up the pack of matches, along with much snow, to the front of his jacket. But he had gained nothing.

After some struggling he managed to get the pack between his mittened hands. In this manner he carried it to his mouth. The ice broke as he opened his mouth with a fierce effort. He used his upper teeth to rub across the pack in order to separate a single match. He succeeded in getting one, which he dropped on his jacket. His condition was no better. He could not pick up the match. Then he thought how he might do it. He picked up the match in his teeth and drew it across his leg. Twenty times he did this before he succeeded in lighting it. As it flamed he held it with his teeth to kindling. But the burning smell went up his nose, causing him to cough. The match fell into the snow and the flame died.

He beat his hands, but failed to produce any feeling in them. Suddenly he bared both hands,

J. Wayne Frye

removing the mittens with his teeth. He caught the whole pack of matches between his hands. His arm muscles were not frozen and he was able to press the hands tightly against the matches. Then he drew the whole pack along his leg. It burst into flame, 70 matches at once! There was no wind to blow them out. He kept his head to one side to escape the burning matches.

He noticed some feeling in his hand. His flesh was burning. He could smell it. The feeling developed into pain. He continued to endure it. He held the flame of the matches to kindling but his hands were taking most of the flame. Finally, when he could endure no more, he pulled his hands apart. The flaming matches fell into the snow, but a small piece if kindling under the brush caught fire.

He began laying dry grasses and the tiniest sticks on the flame. He could not choose carefully because they must be pieces that could be lifted between his hands. Small pieces of green grass stayed on the sticks, and he bit them off as well as he could with his teeth. He treated the flame carefully. It meant life, and it must not cease. The blood had left the surface of his body and he now began to shake from the cold. A large piece of a wet plant fell on the little fire. He tried to push it out with his fingers. His shaking body made him push it too far and he scattered the little fire over a wide space. He tried to push the burning grasses and sticks together again. Even with the strong effort that he made, his trembling fingers would not obey and the sticks were hopelessly scattered. Each stick smoked a little and died.

As he looked about him, his eyes noticed the dog sitting across the ruins of the fire from him. It was making uneasy movements, slightly lifting one foot and then the other. The sight of the dog put a wild idea into his head. He remembered the story of the man, caught in a storm who killed an animal and sheltered himself inside the dead body and thus was saved. He would kill the dog and bury his hands in the warm body until feeling returned to them. Then he could build another fire. He spoke to the dog, calling it to him. But in his voice was a strange note of fear that frightened the animal. It had never known the man to speak in such a tone before. Something was wrong and it sensed danger. It knew not what danger, but somewhere in its brain arose a fear of the man. It flattened its ears at the sound of the man's voice; its uneasy movements and the lifting of its feet became more noticeable. But it would not come to the man. He got down on his hands and knees and went toward the dog. But this unusual position again induced fear and the animal moved away. The man sat in the snow for a moment and struggled for calmness. Then he pulled on his mittens, using his teeth, and stood on his feet. He glanced down to assure himself that he was really standing, because lack of feeling in his feet gave him no relation to the earth. His position, however, removed the fear from the dog's mind.

When he commanded the dog with his usual voice, the dog obeyed and came to him. As it came within his reach, the man lost control. His arms stretched out to hold the dog and he experienced real surprise when he discovered that his hands could not grasp. There was neither bend nor feeling in the fingers. He had forgotten for the moment that they were frozen and that they were freezing more and more. All this happened quickly and before the animal could escape, he encircled its body with his arms. He sat down in the snow, and in this fashion held the dog, while it barked and struggled. But it was all he could do: hold its body encircled in his arms and sit there. He realized that he could not kill the dog. There was no way to do it. With his frozen hands he could neither draw nor hold his knife. Nor could he grasp the dog around the throat. He freed it and it dashed wildly away, still barking.

It stopped 40 feet away and observed him curiously, with ears sharply bent forward. The man looked down at his hands to locate them and found them hanging on the ends of his arms. He thought it curious that it was necessary to use his eyes to discover where his hands were. He began waving his arms, beating the mittened hands against his sides. He did this for five minutes. His heart produced enough blood to stop his shaking. But no feeling was created in his hands. A certain fear of death came upon him. He realized that it was no longer a mere problem of freezing his fingers and toes, or of losing his hands and feet. Now it was a problem of life and death with the circumstances against him. The fear made him lose control of himself and he turned and ran along the creek bed on the old trail. The dog joined him and followed closely behind. The man ran blindly in fear such as he had never known in his life.

Slowly, as he struggled through the snow, he began to see things again—the banks of the creek, the bare trees and the sky. The running made him feel better. He did not shake any more. Maybe, if he continued to run, his feet would stop freezing. Maybe if he ran far enough, he would find the little settlement. Without doubt, he would lose some fingers and toes and some of his face.

There was another thought in his mind that said he would never get to the settlement. It told him that it was too far away, and that the freezing had too great a start and he would soon be dead. He pushed this thought to the back of his mind and refused to consider it. Sometimes it came forward and demanded to be heard. But he pushed it away and tried to think of other things. It seemed strange to him that he could run on feet so frozen that he could not feel them when they struck the earth and took the weight of his body. He seemed to be flying along above the surface and to have no connection with the earth. Several times he caught himself as he was falling. Finally, he dropped to the ground, unable to stop his fall. When he tried to rise, he failed. He must sit and rest, he decided. Next time he would merely walk and keep going. As he sat and regained his breath, he noted that he was feeling warm and comfortable. He was not shaking, and it even seemed that a warm glow had come to his body. And yet, when he touched his nose or face, there was no feeling. Running would not bring life to them. Nor would it help his hands and feet. Then the thought came to him that the frozen portions of his body must be increasing. He tried to keep this thought out of his mind and to forget it. He knew that such thoughts caused a feeling of fright in him and he was afraid of such feelings. But the thought returned and continued, until he could picture his body totally frozen. This was too much, and again he ran wildly along the trail. Once he slowed to a walk, but the thought that the freezing of his body was increasing made him run again. And all the time the dog ran with him, at his heels. When he fell a second time, the dog curled its tail over its feet and sat in front of him, facing him, curiously eager. The warmth and security of the animal angered him. He cursed it until it flattened its ears. This time the shaking because of the cold began more quickly. He was losing his battle with the frost. It was moving into his body from all sides. This thought drove him forward. But he ran no more than 100 feet, when he fell head first.

This was his last moment of fear. When he had recovered his breath and his control, he sat and thought about meeting death with dignity. However, the idea did not come to him in exactly this manner. He was certain to freeze in his present circumstances, and he should accept it calmly. With this newfound peace of mind came the first sleepiness. A good idea, he thought, to sleep his way to death. Freezing was not as bad as people thought. There were many worse ways to die. He pictured a group of people finding his body the next day. Suddenly he saw himself with them, coming along the trail and looking for himself. And, still with them, he came around a turn in the trail and found himself lying in the snow. He did not belong with himself anymore. Even then he was outside of himself, standing with the group and looking at himself in the snow. The dog sat facing him and waiting. The brief day ended in a long evening.

The next day, a group of men came upon a raging fire. They had to turn and run from it. They looked back and saw a man sitting under a tree that was engulfed in flames. The man was also being consumed by flames. Poor soul had put too much debris on the fire and caused himself to catch fire.

THE DAY VADA FRYE DIED

Smiling, my grandmother said, "You see Wayne and Don, fire or ice can be equally dangerous. The man had built a fire to fight the cold, but it wasn't the cold that got him. It was his foolishness in building too big a fire, and as he was being consumed by that fire, he had delusions about the cold. You boys should have no delusions about what you did being wrong. You must be careful if you build a fire. You see life is like a fire. If you do not control your life, it, like a fire, will burn out of control. Be wise enough to know when a fire is getting out of hand."

--

At the time, we felt lucky that neither of us got a spanking, but we also were perplexed that we had to sit through that long story just for my grandmother to make a point, a point that was probably lost on us at the time. Now, I realize the cold was a metaphor for a life filled with challenges that will test our souls, and you have to be careful the way you meet those challenges, because just like the man who built too big a fire to combat the cold, you might allow a fire to get out of control.

The truth was that my grandmother was a force of nature. She was like a raging inferno of knowledge setting a fire in the forest at night when no one else is awake. However, she knew how to control the fire. She knew how to accept the foibles of youth and embrace the idea that growing up was a learning process that often involved doing totally stupid things. She knew Don and I had to live in our own flames that would sometimes burn too bright and too wild, and she just wanted to make sure we did not let the fires we built get out of control.

Chapter 5
Better to be Miserable With Money
Than Without It

Vada Frye knew
The power of love,
Standing by her grandson
When push came to shove.

Wholeheartedly,
She loved me,
And inspired me
With true devotion.

It was a blessing
To have been her grandson,
To have been loved

THE DAY VADA FRYE DIED

Without any conditions.

Her words of wisdom
Opened my eyes
To the world
And to myself.

By seeing the best in me,
She empowered me.
By believing in me,
She transformed me.

She grew old
And floated away,
But her love remains standing
Eternally by my side.

As I sat heartbroken by her bedside reflecting on the many stories my grandmother told me and my cousins, I pondered how much I was going to miss her use of storytelling to elevate moral clarity. How could life ever be the same with her gone? It absolutely could not be. I know that fact as an old man now who all these years has never had a single day go by that I did not think of her and her love. No, not one single day. Living without her has been tolerable, but had she been around life would have been so much better, especially at times when I desperately needed comforting. Nobody could lend comfort the way she did. She was comfort! She was home. She was salvation.

J. Wayne Frye

THE DAY VADA FRYE DIED

As I looked at her wrinkled and weathered face, placing my hand on top of hers, I could not shed any tears, because our love for one another called for no tears. It called for joy that we had been able to share so much time together, so much love.

I was a young man who was suddenly in a tiny boat on an angry ocean of despair. Some boats eventually float ashore. And some boats, like mine, seemed to float farther and farther from the land I had known, the safe harbour of my grandmother's love. I uttered the words: "Grandmother, please don't leave me" over and over again and again. I truly believed that she would not leave me, because she knew I needed her so desperately.

My grandmother lived her life as a force for kindness, compassion, fairness, character, benevolence and for true good. Whatever I possessed of those qualities was because she imparted them to me.

She looked so tired and weary lying there in a coma. Night was falling upon her life, but to me she was only sleeping, or had she finally come to the end of life's journey? I looked out the hospital window and the pale moon was just rising. I sensed a far off horizon where the eternal night waited for her. Time was about to cease for her, but for me cherished memories would still linger until I walked into that eternal night myself. Would my final thoughts as I walked that final path be of her?

THE DAY VADA FRYE DIED

When the brain becomes too tired, as mine had, the mind stops decrypting the perceptions of the mental world and surrenders thought willingly to the grand moments of life that rest comfortably in the back of the brain, waiting to be called up in the crystal clarity of the present. The safeguards of my thinking patterns were starting to weaken, and I realized that when a star dies, it, no doubt, reflects back on its bright dreams, as I was reflecting on my dreams that I had shared with my grandmother.

I started to think of something I once told my grandmother about money, because we lived in America, where the greatest God of all for most people was money. I once told her that I was always hearing that money doesn't bring happiness. She said, "Let me tell you a story about money Wayne."

The Power of Money Story (Her story, my words.)

Anthony Rockwell, who had made millions of dollars by making and selling Rockwall's soap, stood at a window of his large Fifth Avenue house in Manhattan. He was looking out at his neighbour, G. Van Schuylight Suffolk-Jones. This neighbour was a proud member of a proud old New York family. He came out of his door and got into a cab. He looked once quickly, as usual, at Anthony Rockwall's house. The look showed that Suffolk-Jones was a very important man, while a rich soap maker was nothing.

"I will have this house painted red, white, and blue next summer," said the Soap King to himself. "And we'll see how he likes that." And then Anthony Rockwell turned around and shouted, "Mike!" in a loud voice. He never used a bell to call a servant. "Tell my son," he said when the servant came, "to come to me before he leaves the house."

When young Rockwell entered the room, the old man put down the newspaper he had been reading. "Richard," said Anthony Rockwell, "what do you pay for the soap that you use?"

Richard had finished college six months before, and he had come home to live. He had not yet learned to understand his father. He was always being surprised by him. He said, "Six dollars for twelve pieces."

"And your clothes?" the old man asked.

"About sixty dollars, usually."

"You are a gentleman," said his father. "I have heard of young men who pay twenty-four dollars for twelve pieces of soap, and more than a hundred for clothes. You have as much money to throw away as anyone else has. But what you do is reasonable. I myself use Rockwell Soap, because it is the best. When you pay more than ten cents for a piece of soap, you are paying for a sweet strong smell and a name. But fifty cents is good for a young man like you. You are a gentleman. People say that if a man is not a gentleman his son can't be a gentleman; but perhaps his son's son will be a gentleman. But they are wrong. Money does it faster than that. Money has made you a gentleman. It has almost made me a gentleman. I have become very much like the two gentlemen who own the houses on each side of us. My manners are now almost as good as theirs. But they still can't sleep at night because a soap maker lives in this house."

"There are some things that money can't do," said the young man rather sadly.

"Don't say that," said old Anthony. "Money is successful every time. I don't know anything you can't buy with it. Tell me something that money can't buy. And I want you to tell me something more. Something is wrong with you. I've seen it for two weeks. Tell me. Let me help you. In twenty-four hours I could have eleven million dollars here in my hands. Are you sick?"

"Some people call it sickness."

"Oh!" said Anthony. "What's her name? Why don't you ask her to marry you? She would be glad to do it. You have money, you are good-looking, and you are a good boy. Your hands are clean. You have no dirt on them."

"I haven't had a chance to ask her," said Richard Rockwell.

"Make a chance," said Anthony. "Take her for a walk in the park. Or walk home with her from church."

"You don't know the life of a rich girl, father. Every hour and minute of her time is planned. I must have her, or the world is worth nothing to me. And I can't write to say I love her. I can't do that."

THE DAY VADA FRYE DIED

"Do you tell me," said the old man, "that with all my money you can't get an hour or two of a girl's time?"

"I've waited too long. She's going to Europe the day after tomorrow. She's going to be there two years. I'm allowed to see her alone tomorrow evening for a few minutes. She's coming to the city on a train. I'm going to meet her with a cab. Then we'll drive fast to the theatre where she must meet her mother and some other people. Do you think she would listen to me then? No. Or in the theatre? No. Or after the theatre? No! No, father, this is one trouble that your money can't help. We can't buy one minute of time with money. If we could, rich people would live longer. There's no hope of talking with Miss Lantry before she sails."

"Richard, my boy," said old Anthony, "I'm glad you're not really sick. You say money won't buy time? Perhaps it won't buy all of time, but I've seen it buy some little pieces."

That evening the old Anthony's sister, Ellen, came to Anthony, to talk about the troubles that lovers have.

"He told me all about it," said Anthony. "I told him he could have all the money he wanted. Then he began to say that money was no use to him. He said money couldn't help."

"Oh, Anthony," said Ellen, "I wish you wouldn't think so much of money. Money is no help for love. Love is all powerful. If he had only spoken to her earlier! She could never say no to our Richard. But now I fear it is too late. All your gold cannot buy happiness for your son."

At eight the next evening Ellen took an old gold ring and gave it to Richard. "Wear it tonight," she said. "Your mother gave it to me. She asked me to give it to you when you had found the girl you loved."

Young Rockwell took the ring and tried to put it on his little finger. It was too small. He put it inside his coat, in a place where he thought it would be safe. And then he called for his cab. At the station he met Miss Lantry.

"We must not keep my mother and the others waiting," said she.

"To Wallack's Theater as fast as you can drive," said Richard to the cabby.

They rolled along Forty-Second Street to Broadway and from there to Thirty-Fourth Street. Then young Richard quickly ordered the cabby to stop. "I've dropped a ring," he said, getting out. "It was my mother's and I don't want to lose it. This will take only a minute. I saw where it fell."

In less than a minute he was again in the cab with the ring. But within that minute, a wagon had stopped in front of the cab. The cabby tried to pass on the left, but a cab was there. He tried to pass on the right, but another cab was there. He could not go back. He was caught where he was and could not move in any direction. These sudden stops of movement will happen in the city. Instead of moving along the street in their usual orderly way, all the wagons and cabs will suddenly be mixed together and stopped.

"Why don't you drive farther?" said Miss Lantry. "We'll be late."

Richard stood up in the cab and looked around. He saw a stream of cabs and wagons and everything else on wheels rolling toward the corner where Broadway, Sixth Avenue and Thirty-Fourth Street met. They came from all directions. And more and more were rolling toward them. More and more were caught there. Drivers and cabbies shouted. Everyone on wheels in New York City seemed to be hurrying to this place.

"I'm very sorry," said Richard. He sat down again. "We can't move. They won't get this straight in an hour. If I hadn't dropped the ring, we—"

"Let me see the ring," said Miss Lantry. "Since we really can't hurry because of the traffic jam. I don't care. I didn't want to go to the theatre. I don't like the theatre."

At eleven that night someone stopped at the door of Anthony's room. "Come in," shouted Anthony. He had been reading and he put down his book. It was Ellen. "They are going to be married Anthony," she said. "She has promised to marry our Richard. On their way to the theatre their cab was stopped in the street. It was two hours before it could move again. And my dear brother Anthony, don't ever talk about the power of money again. It was a little ring, a true love ring that was the cause of our Richard finding his happiness. He dropped it in the street and had to get out and find it. And before they could continue, the cab was caught among the others. He told her of his love there in the cab. Money is nothing, Anthony. True love is everything."

"I'm glad the boy got what he wanted," said old Anthony. "I told him I didn't care how much money—"

"But, brother Anthony, what could your money do?"

"Sister," said Anthony Rockwell. "I'm reading a book with a good story in it. It's a wild adventure story, but I like it. And I want to find what happens next. I wish you would let me go on reading."

My grandmother said, "The story should end right here. I wish it would. I'm sure you too wish it would end here my dear Wayne, and we would both see that love conquers all and that no amount of money can buy love. But we must go further with the story to reveal the truth."

"You see, the next day a person whose name was Kelly came to Anthony Rockwell's house to see him. He said to Anthony, "It cost more than I expected. I got the cabs, most of them, for $5, but some I had to pay $10, and I had to pay the most to the cops, $50 each. But didn't it work beautifully, Mr. Rockwell? They were all on time. And it was two hours before anyone could move. All together, I spent the $5000 you gave me, plus $300 of my own money."

Anthony said, "O.K. here is the $1000 I promised you for arranging the traffic jam and the extra $300 that you paid out-of-pocket." A sly grin crept across Anthony's lips as he realized how mush power he had because of money. He continued, "Creating that traffic jam will bring happiness to my son, a happiness I am thankful I had the money to arrange."

--

Then my grandmother would always get that usual look of satisfaction on her face that crept across it when she thought she had taught me a lesson that would require me to think, a lesson that would stay with me the rest of my life. That was the purpose of all her stories, even fairy tales when I was a child. She grinned what Tom Morello, the famous singer, guitarist and social activist would call a Cheshire grin. She said in her usual soft voice, "So, you see Wayne, when people tell you that money cannot buy happiness, remember that in some cases it can. My own mother and father often told me that money can't buy happiness, but I can definitely tell you that if you are going to be miserable it is better to be miserable with money than without it."

The day she told me that story was one of the many days when the stories brought a gradual, often over days, weeks, months and years a clarity to what she had said, a clarity that was like a seed planted into the ground that grew into a mighty tree of knowledge.

So much of what my grandmother said over the years was said because she wanted me to grasp the real world, the substantial image of actuality which her soul so constantly beheld. She wanted me to seek truth and not be caught in the darkness of ignorance that keeps so many people locked in a prison of their own making. I firmly believe that she understood that as I digested her musings that they would fade into something impalpable under my eyes and ears, then in a moment of aforementioned clarity that could be days, weeks, months or years away they would be manifested, and I would be transfigured with an understanding of their true meaning. Weakness, decrepitude, timidity and inexperience would fall from me in that magic moment of glorious realization of the profundity of what she had once said.

Even today, when I hear people, especially rich, self-absorbed individuals who want to keep the masses fooled, say *"Money can't buy you happiness"* I remember those words of my grandmother which I always repeated in every single marketing class I taught when a university professor, "Oh, but if you are going to be miserable, it is better to be miserable with money than without it."

THE DAY VADA FRYE DIED

Chapter 7
Angel of Death Who Had Come Knocking

People you love never die,
Not completely.
They live in your mind
The way they always did.
You keep their light alive.
If you remember them well enough,
They can still guide you,
Like the shine of long-extinguished stars
Can guide ships in unfamiliar waters.

My grandmother was uneducated, but that did not alter the fact that she was an astute observer of life; and thereby, was able to comprehend things that even well-educated individuals could not understand. She could probably not even define capitalism, but she understood its deeply inherent evil which promoted the glory of greed; and thereby, relegated a large swath of individuals and their children to be constantly mired in poverty. Experiencing the Great Depression first hand, she comprehended the failures of an economic system that collapsed in the 1930's and brought ruin and hunger to so many. I am sure she probably never even heard of Karl Marx, who believed in the dialectic process, the primacy, the inevitable, the irresistible transformative power of the grand sweep of history and of large events, even when it seemed like the powers-that-be of the existing socioeconomic and political order held all the cards. While nothing succeeds like success, as the seemingly winning situation of the moment always proceeds for the privileged class, I do believe she understood that after time arrogance, hubris, and an intense feeling of invulnerable invincibility that karma would hopefully cause the mighty to fall. I was generally too young to understand it at the time, but I believe many of her stories analyzed the sowing of the seeds of future mistakes, miscalculations and eventual disaster for the privileged class that remained stubbornly blind to needs of the poor. I believe she longed for the final crisis, and the cascade of events that would eventually sweep aside the privileged establishment that completely controlled the socioeconomic and political order.

She would often tell me that man was a beast, probably the worst of the animal kingdom. Alone among primates, man killed for sport or lust or greed. He would murder his brother to possess his brother's land. She said that evil breeds evil in great numbers, and she was an environmentalist and didn't even know it, because she believed man would make a desert out of his home and others homes by destroying trees, the soil, the water and all things needed to enjoy a good life in the name of profit. She said that this evil would drive man back into the jungle lair, for the privileged class was the harbinger of death. (*Words altered to make it more understandable to the reader.*)

As I looked at her labouring to breathe, I reflected on so much she had taught me, often without even knowing she was giving me a lesson in living that I would carry with me forever. She had endured great hardship in her life, but she and Dixon Frye had faced those hardships and survived the greatest economic upheaval in American history created by the barons of greed on Wall Street – the Great Depression. She had told me in her own way how the system of greed left the poor dirty with the grime of working for peanuts, ugly with the burden of having to struggle for sustenance and so tired that there was no fight left in any of the poor to make a stand against the evil of such an

THE DAY VADA FRYE DIED

oppressive economic system. Again, not in her words but in mine, she conveyed the idea that in fighting this system of economic slavery she felt like a marshmallow heading into a house fire armed with a cup of water and a saltine cracker. The working men and women were born into a system of slavery to the privileged class, and their children and their children's children would suffer the same fate in a system that had no heart or soul and allowed only limited upward mobility to keep the masses believing that everybody had an equal chance.

She could see the vast majority of people falling for the illusion of prosperity; and thereby, swallowing the intense propaganda gobbledegook that was preached by a government that served the interests of the privileged class, but needed the working class to keep their cash registers ringing.

I was thoroughly tired from sitting there hour after hour, but I could not leave her, could not stop pleading with her to please not leave me. There was some primal force keeping me awake, forging within me an iron will not to leave her side. I didn't exactly lie awake, but I didn't exactly sleep either. As soon as I shut my eyes I could see in my mind a slow moving river gathering strength with the currents riding in at first picking up straws and dead leaves and little sticks, and then boards and pieces of firewood and whole logs. It gradually became a roaring tempest headed to the sea, the water rising and filling all the airy spaces of fields and woods, carrying away everything that would float, casting up the people on the shore and scattering them, scattering or drowning their animals and poultry flocks along with them. The whole world it seemed was cast adrift, riding the currents, whirled about in eddies, and the old life submerged and gone forever as my dear grandmother was leaving me. She could not leave me. I would not let her go. "Oh please," I whispered in her left ear, "don't leave me. Please don't leave me."

I was 22, but I still had the mind of a child, because I longed for the safety I felt in her arms, the safety of knowing someone cared more for me than anyone else in the world, the safety offered by a woman who never wavered in her devotion to me and my welfare. I kept asking myself why I left her to visit my fiancé. Why couldn't I have the sanctity of saying goodbye? She was not ill when I left, but she was not her usual self. There was a spark that was usually there which was missing when I pulled out of her driveway and she waved goodbye to me. There was an emptiness that I felt as I cruised out onto the highway. I should have turned around and gone back. Why didn't I?

I began to plead with her to wake up at least, if for no other reason to simply say goodbye. Still there were no tears, and I wondered why I was not crying. Why I was not bawling like a baby, because I was losing more than I had ever lost in my life. I had cried when my grandfather died, and I certainly did not have the depth of relationship with him that I did with my grandmother.

There simply is no diversity in longing for those we love. There is no revolution without determined devotion to the cause. There simply is no justice without inconvenience. There is no development of character without flaws. There is no dignity without respect. There is no learning without fear of failing. There is no love without heartbreak. There is no path through the tangled wood of life without the thorns. There is no dream without an occasional nightmare. There is no determination without doubtfulness. Only those who have felt excruciating pain can understand the pain of others. My pain at that moment was as real as any I had ever felt. Its depth was like carelessly diving into an endless ocean knowing that you could not make any shore, but still hoping against hope that you would somehow avoid sinking into the depths of murky water that lay before you.

He who truly learns must suffer. And even in our sleep, pain that cannot forget falls drop by drop upon the heart, and in our own despair, often against our will, comes wisdom and the realization that death is as inevitable as dew in the morning of discontent.

Take this kiss upon the brow!

THE DAY VADA FRYE DIED

And, in parting from you now,
Thus much let me avow —
You are not wrong, who deem
That my days have been a dream;
Yet if hope has flown away
In a night, or in a day,
In a vision, or in none,
Is it therefore the less gone?
All that we see or seem
Is but a dream within a dream.

I stand amid the roar
Of a surf-tormented shore,
And I hold within my hand
Grains of the golden sand —
How few! Yet how they creep
Through my fingers to the deep,
While I weep — while I weep!
O my! Can I not grasp
Them with a tighter clasp?
O my! Can I not save
One from the pitiless wave?
Is all that we see or seem
But a dream within a dream?

I knew that her spirit which had gone forth to shape my world and make it live was still alive. I just had no doubt. I could see that I lived in her created world, and it was still being created as she lay on the bed of death. She would be part of my world forever. There was no escape from the influence she had on that world in which I lived. Her spirit that made it whole for me would always be constantly shaping it and reshaping it.

I remembered, as I gazed down at her, one of the most poignant stories she had told me about the power of love for the least of us in a world that so often neglected the needs of those we only saw in passing, a world where disregard for the power of the lowly to rise up and make a difference was neglected while we praised the rich, the famous, the exalted without the realization that the "real people" who make a "real difference" die alone, unheralded and unappreciated for their contributions to the welfare of humanity. As I continued looking down at her, that story crystallized in my mind. It was one of the favourite stories she told me. In fact, she told and retold it many times, and I would often see moisture in her eyes after she finished it, because she saw in it some deeper meaning than my young mind could not comprehend, maybe because she had seen death so often in her life. One time when she told it we had been talking of her brother Grady, who, one night when riding a horse to visit his girlfriend, was thrown to the ground by a bucking frightened horse, hitting a rock with his head. He was found by a friend and brought home, where he lay in a coma for weeks, finally dying. That was one of many nights I saw her near tears as she reflected on the love she had for a brother she lost so long ago.

The Masterpiece (Retold in my words.)

In a little district west of Washington Square the streets have run crazy and broken themselves into small strips called "places." These "places" make strange angles and curves. One Street crosses itself a time or two. An artist once discovered a valuable possibility in this street. Suppose a collector with a bill for paints, paper and canvas should, in traversing this route, suddenly meet himself coming back, without a cent having been paid on account!

So, to quaint old Greenwich Village the art people soon came prowling, hunting for north windows and eighteenth-century gables and Dutch attics and low rents. Then they imported some pewter mugs and a chafing dish or two from Sixth Avenue, and became a "colony."

At the top of a squatty, three-story brick Sue and Johnsy had their studio. "Johnsy" was a nom de plume for Joanna. One was from Maine; the other from California. They had met at the still standing today restaurant Delmonico's, and found their tastes in art so congenial that the joint studio apartment where they now lived resulted.

That was in May. In November a cold, unseen stranger, whom the doctors called pneumonia, stalked about the colony, touching one here and there with its icy fingers. Over on the east side this ravager strode boldly, smiting its victims by scores, but its feet trod slowly, though still deliberately.

Mr. Pneumonia was not what you would call a chivalric old gentleman. A mite of a little woman with blood thinned by California zephyrs was hardly fair game for the red-fisted, short-breathed old duffer. But Johnsy he smote; and she lay, scarcely moving, on her painted iron bedstead, looking through the small Dutch window-panes at the blank side of the next brick house across the courtyard.

One morning the busy doctor invited Sue into the hallway looking at her as his shaggy, grey eyebrows rose in dismay. "She has one chance in - let us say, ten," he said, as he shook down the mercury in his clinical thermometer. "And that chance is for her to want to live. This way people have of lining-up on the side of the undertaker is apparent on people who too easily give up. Your little lady friend has made up her mind that she's not going to get well. Has she anything on her mind?"

"She - she wanted to paint the Bay of Naples some day." said Sue.

"Paint? My goodness, dear! Has she anything on her mind worth thinking twice - a man for instance?"

"A man?" said Sue, with a high pitched twang in her voice that actually toned a disdain for those creatures of the opposite sex. "Is a man worth - but, no, doctor; there is nothing of the kind."

THE DAY VADA FRYE DIED

"Well, it is the weakness, then," said the doctor. "I will do all that science, so far as it may filter through my efforts, can accomplish. But whenever my patient begins to count the carriages in her funeral procession I subtract 50 per cent from the curative power of medicines. If you will get her spirits up enough to fight, I will promise you a one-in-five chance for her, instead of one in ten. It is as if she wants to die. You must work to elevate her spirits and her willpower."

After the doctor had gone, Sue went into the workroom and cried. Then she swaggered into Johnsy's room with her drawing board, whistling ragtime. Johnsy lay, scarcely making a ripple under the bedclothes, with her face toward the window. Sue stopped whistling, thinking she was asleep.

She arranged her board and began a pen-and-ink drawing to illustrate a magazine story. As Sue was sketching a pair of elegant horseshow riding trousers and a monocle of the figure of the hero, an Idaho cowboy, she heard a low sound, several times repeated. She went quickly to Sue's bedside.

Johnsy's eyes were open wide. She was looking out the window and counting - counting backward. "Twelve," she said, and little later "eleven"; and then "ten," and "nine"; and then "eight" and "seven", almost together.

Sue look solicitously out of the window. What was there to count? There was only a bare, dreary yard to be seen, and the blank side of the brick house twenty feet away. An old ivy vine, gnarled and decayed at the roots, climbed half way up the brick wall. The cold breath of autumn had stricken its leaves from the vine until its skeleton branches clung, almost bare, to the crumbling bricks.

"What is it, dear? What is preying so heavily on your mind?" asked Sue.

"Six," said Johnsy, in almost a whisper. "They're falling faster now. Three days ago there were almost a hundred. It made my head ache to count them. But now it's easy. There goes another one. There are only five left now."

"Five what, dear? Tell me."

"Leaves. On the ivy vine. When the last one falls I must go, too. I've known that for three days. Didn't the doctor tell you?"

"Oh, I never heard of such nonsense," complained Sue, with magnificent scorn. "What have old ivy leaves to do with your getting well? And you used to love that vine so, you naughty girl. Don't be a silly. Why, the doctor told me this morning that your chances for getting well real soon were very good. Try to take some broth now, and let me go back to my drawing."

"You needn't get any broth," said Johnsy, keeping her eyes fixed out the window. "There goes another. That leaves just four. I want to see the last one fall before it gets dark. Then I'll go, too."

THE DAY VADA FRYE DIED

"Johnsy, dear," said Sue, bending over her, "will you promise me to keep your eyes closed, and not look out the window until I am done working? I must hand these drawings in by tomorrow. I need the light, or I would draw the shade down."

"Couldn't you draw in the other room?" asked Johnsy, coldly.

"I'd rather be here by you," said Sue. "Besides, I don't want you to keep looking at those silly ivy leaves."

"Tell me as soon as you have finished," said Johnsy, closing her eyes, and lying white and still, "because I want to see the last one fall. I'm tired of waiting. I'm tired of thinking. I want to turn loose my hold on everything and go sailing down, down, just like one of those poor, tired leaves."

"Try to sleep," said Sue. "I must call Mr. Behrman up from his apartment to be my model for the old hermit miner drawing I am doing for a magazine. I'll not be gone a minute. Don't try to move 'til I come back."

Old Behrman was a painter who lived on the ground floor beneath them. He was past sixty and had a thick beard curling down from his chin which stood out markedly with his impish-like body. Behrman was a failure in art. All his life he had wielded the brush without any success. He had been always about to paint a masterpiece, but had never yet begun it. For several years he had painted nothing except items deemed appropriate for commerce or advertising. He earned a little by serving as a model to those young artists in the area who could not pay the price of a professional. He drank gin to excess, and still talked of his coming masterpiece. He was a fierce and grumpy little old man, who scoffed terribly at softness in anyone, but seemed to have a soft spot for Sue and Johnsy.

Sue found Behrman smelling strongly of gin in his dimly lighted den below. In one corner was a blank canvas on an easel that had been waiting there for twenty-five years to receive the first line of the masterpiece. She told him of Johnsy's fancy, and how she feared she would, indeed, light and fragile as a leaf herself, float away, when her slight hold upon the world grew weaker as the last leaf fell.

Old Behrman, with his red eyes plainly streaming, shouted his contempt and derision for such idiotic imaginings. "Poppycock!" he cried. "Surely she cannot be so idiotic."

"I know," replied Sue. "However, will you please pose for me while I still have sunlight?"

"I will," replied the inebriated Behrman. "But what are we to do about Johnsy?"

"She is very ill and weak," said Sue, "and the fever has left her mind morbid."

"Go on" offered discombobulated Behrman, "I shall come with you for half an hour to pose. Then I must come back downstairs and work on my masterpiece."

THE DAY VADA FRYE DIED

Sue had wearied of always hearing about his masterpiece. She simply said, "Okay, please let's go upstairs, and I'll draw you quickly."

Johnsy was sleeping when they went upstairs. Sue pulled the shade down to the window-sill, and motioned Behrman into the other room. In there they peered out the window fearfully at the ivy vine. Then they looked at each other for a moment without speaking. A persistent, cold rain was falling, mingled with snow. Behrman, in his old blue shirt, took his seat as the hermit miner on an upturned kettle for a rock and Sue did her drawing.

When Sue awoke from a restless nights' sleep the next morning she found Johnsy with dull, wide-open eyes staring at the drawn green shade.

"Pull it up; I want to see," she ordered, in a whisper.

Wearily Sue obeyed. But, lo! After the beating rain and fierce gusts of wind that had endured through the livelong night, there yet stood out against the brick wall one ivy leaf. It was the last one on the vine. Still dark green near its stem, with its serrated edges tinted with the yellow of dissolution and decay, it hung bravely from the branch some twenty feet above the ground.

"It is the last one," said Johnsy. "I thought it would surely fall during the night. I heard the wind. It will fall today, and I shall die at the same time."

THE DAY VADA FRYE DIED

"Dear, dear!" said Sue, leaning her worn face down to the pillow, "think of me, if you won't think of yourself. What would I do?"

Johnsy did not answer. The loneliest thing in the entire world is a soul when it is making ready to go on its mysterious, ending journey. The lack of a will to live seemed to possess her more strongly as one by one the ties that bound her to friendship and to earth were loosed.

The day wore away, and even through the twilight they could see the lone ivy leaf clinging to its stem against the wall. And then, with the coming of the night the north wind was again loosed, while the rain still beat against the windows and pattered down from above.

When it was light enough Johnsy, the merciless, commanded that the shade be raised. The ivy leaf was still there.

Johnsy lay for a long time looking at it. And then she called to Sue, who was stirring her chicken broth over the gas stove.

"I've been a silly girl, Sue," said Johnsy. "Something has made that last leaf stay there to show me how ridiculous I was. I do not want to die. You may bring me a little broth now, and something to drink, and no; bring me a hand-mirror first, and then pack some pillows about me, and I will sit up and watch you cook. And hour later she said, "Sue, some day I hope to paint the Bay of Naples."

The doctor came in the afternoon, and Sue made an excuse to go into the hallway as he left.

THE DAY VADA FRYE DIED

"Even chances," said the doctor, taking Sue's thin, shaking hand in his. "With good nursing she'll live." And now I must see another case I have downstairs. Behrman, his name is - some kind of an artist, I believe. Pneumonia, too. He is an old, weak man, and the attack is acute. There is no hope for him; but he goes to the hospital today to be made more comfortable."

The next day the doctor said to Sue: "She's out of danger. You can relax now."

That afternoon Sue came to the bed where Johnsy lay, contentedly knitting a very blue and very useless woollen shoulder scarf, and put one arm around her, pillows and all. "I have something to tell you," she said. "Mr. Behrman died of pneumonia today in the hospital. He was ill only two days. The janitor found him the morning of the first day in his room downstairs helpless with pain. His shoes and clothing were wet through and icy cold. They couldn't imagine where he had been on such a dreadful night. And then they found a lantern, still lighted, and a ladder that had been dragged from its place, and some scattered brushes, and a palette with green and yellow colours mixed on it, and look out the window, dear, at the last ivy leaf on the wall. Didn't you wonder why it never fluttered or moved when the wind blew? Ah, darling, it's Behrman's masterpiece. He painted it there the night that the last leaf fell. Yes, he finally painted his masterpiece."

THE DAY VADA FRYE DIED

That was one of her stories I have told and retold, because it proved that there is one masterpiece we all have in us – love.

Recalling the tale put a smile on my face, because I remembered how much she loved telling the story. It was definitely one of her favourites.

Watching someone you love battle against death is the height of emotional pain. There are no words for just how broken it made me feel. It was like waking up from a bad dream only to find out that the dream was better than the waking nightmare of reality I had to face. It was like watching the sunlight of hope fade from the sky, like watching death suck the one you love dry and being totally powerless to stop it. I realized my helplessness, which is why I kept saying, "Please don't leave me." However, I was coming to the realization that I might as well try to stop the waves from rolling in, or the sun from setting. In the end, the waves will roll, the sun will set, and death will come. Yet, I kept begging her not to give into the angel of death who had come knocking.

Chapter 7
Defying Convention for the Sake of Love

Having a grandmother is like having an army.
This is a grandchild's ultimate privilege:
Knowing that someone is on your side,
Always, whatever the details,
Even when you are wrong.
A grandmother is both a sword and a shield.

Vada Frye was born in 1899, and her grandmother remembered the Civil War in the USA (1861-1865). So, it was common for people like my grandmother to accept segregation (separation of races) as the norm. Yet, even though prejudice was taught and almost universally accepted in the Southern

THE DAY VADA FRYE DIED

USA, she was a woman, despite a lack of education, who acquired great knowledge as she aged, and in the process began to comprehend the evil of a society that taught hatred for people of colour. In fact, I was taught the same hatred, and accepted it for most of my young life, but my grandmother and I both began to question the validity of the idea that one race was superior to the other.

Brainwashing is actually incredibly easy, especially when it is done to the young. That is why school children in the USA were forced to stand and say the pledge of allegiance every morning in school until the Supreme Court ruled in West Virginia Board of Education vs. Barnette in 1943 that the Free Speech clause of the First Amendment prohibits public schools from forcing students to salute the American flag and say the Pledge of Allegiance. Despite this ruling, to this very day all schools across America say the Pledge every morning, but they cannot force any student to say it. Yet, there is obviously great psychological pressure put on individuals to join their peers in reciting it. I continued to say the pledge for years until I got to high school and my rebellious nature prevailed and I refused to acquiesce to brain washing. As alluded to earlier, this got me in trouble. Ironically, years later when I was Director of Intensive Academic Studies for gang kids in South-central Los Angeles I was appalled that when I would take my charges, which numbered 400, into the massive auditorium where 2000 students were assembled, the presiding principal would actually tell the kids to stand for the pledge of allegiance. I informed by students and their teachers that they did not have to stand or say the Pledge. Of course, if they wanted to do so, they could. I was called into the Los Angeles Schools Superintendent's office and told that my students were required to recite the pledge. I whipped out a pocket copy of the 1943 Supreme Court decision and tossed it on the superintendent's desk and walked out. I never heard from him again, and my students never stood again or recited the Pledge. My bold nature in standing up for right was a result of my grandmother teaching me to never bow before injustice.

Americans are the most brainwashed people in the world, and since the emergence of the MAGA crowd, it is now a nation on an unrelenting march backward.

Fortunately, when I was young, I had parents and grandparents who refused to accept the tyranny of religious and political fascists. My parents and my grandparents on my father's side taught me to think for myself, and people who think for themselves are a danger to the establishment and the privileged class.

Still, when I was young, on Sunday mornings my grandparents, after I begged, allowed me to attend church. They did not have to bother taking me, because the churches sent buses to pick up children for Sunday school. I remember once asking my grandfather why the church sent out buses to pick up children for Sunday school. I still vividly recall his pointed reply, "Because son, they need to get you while you are young, so they can fill you with fear. If 'un it was up to me you wouldn't be going to that place where they spend more time preaching hate than love, but your grandmother says its okay for you to go, so I let her have her way. Just between you and me, them people ain't preaching nothing I wanna hear. Anyway, I stopped believing in fairy tales when I was about five. You can go, but just remember to never let nobody do your thinking for you. You got yourself a pretty good brain from what have seen. Just be sure you use it."

I did not stop going to Sunday school after that conversation with my grandfather, because my grandmother took me aside and said, "Your granddaddy ain't got no use for religion, and I ain't trying to influence you one way or another, so you go on to church cause I know you go to be with other kids and to play games. What your granddaddy is telling you is that you can't believe everything that's written in the Bible. Just remember you gotta a brain – use it."

I cannot be sure if my grandfather was an atheist, but I believe, from his actions and open disdain for religion, he probably was at a time when being so was not something you openly proclaimed, especially in the southern USA, sometimes called the Bible Belt, because questioning the Bible was something that was not done in public.

My grandmother, although she attended church maybe 5 or 6 times a year, I believe went for socialization and to commune with family, not to embrace religion. The southern church even taught that segregation was part of God's plan and that Black people were cast out because they were of the tribe of Ham. I can remember hearing ministers actually promote the idea that Blacks, by their very nature, were evil and had been cast out by God and sent to live in Africa. This biblical story has been the single greatest justification for Black slavery for hundreds of years. It is a strange justification indeed, for there is no reference to it in regards to Blacks at all in the Bible. And yet just about everyone, especially in the American South, understood that in this story God meant to curse black Africans with eternal slavery, the so-called Curse of Ham. As one proslavery author wrote in 1838, "The blacks were originally designed to vassalage by the Patriarch Noah." So the slavery of black people was justified by God! My grandmother would often discuss this and tell me it was all propaganda by pro-segregation politicians. In fact, she once recited a poem to me that summed up the whole situation.

Southern trees bear a strange fruit,
Blood on the leaves and blood at the root

THE DAY VADA FRYE DIED

Black bodies swinging in the breeze,
Strange fruit hanging from the poplar trees.

I never personally witnessed a lynching, but there were still lynchings in the south when I was a child. I vividly recall the incident of Emmett Till. The murder of the 14-year-old African-American brought attention to the racial violence and injustice prevalent in Mississippi and the rest of the south. While visiting his relatives, Till went to the Bryant store with his cousins, and may have whistled at Carolyn Bryant, who was white. Her husband, Roy Bryant, and brother-in-law, J.W. Milam, kidnapped and brutally murdered Till, dumping his body in the Tallahatchie River. Both men were acquitted by an all-white jury.

I can recall my grandmother demonstratively fussing at the television screen when the story of his murder flashed on the news. She turned to me and said, "I was taught to hate coloured people, but they is no excuse for anyone killing a 14 year old boy over nonsense. If a white boy had whistled at the woman, wouldn't nothing be thought about it. I tell you, Wayne, this just ain't right."

I could see she was emotionally distraught over what had happened. She looked at me, and said, "You know I got a newspaper article about a lynching in Vance County in 1933. I cut it out and saved it. I always thought you were too young to see it, but I think you need to see it, 'cause you need to learn about how evil white people who hate Negroes can be. This has to stop, Wayne. It is an evil that has gone on for too long."

She walked back to her bedroom and came out carrying a dilapidated cigar box containing a batch of old newspaper articles she had cut out and folded. Rummaging through them, she brought one out and handed it to me. I still have it today in a box of what I call grandmother memories.

Staring at the picture, for the first time in my life I actually had an inkling of the horror faced by people of colour in the south where I lived. I looked at the picture and uttered no words, but my grandmother had words to say. "You live in a part of the world where people live in fear Wayne, and it ain't just Negroes who live in fear. The white folks are scared too, scared that if they are friendly with Negroes or take a stand against the way they are treated by white folks they are gonna suffer the same fate as Negroes. I know you seen people in Klan outfits around Asheboro, and the Ku Klux Klan is a bunch of idiots that wanna cover their faces, because they know what they are doing is wrong."

She was right, I was friends with many children whose fathers were in the Klan, and actually paraded around in their uniforms, proudly displaying their ignorance. It was an ignorance wilfully passed on from father to son.

I kept talking about what happened to Emmett Till, telling my grandmother that I had grown weary of the arrogance of white people who always looked with disfavour on Blacks. She looked at me with a sense of pride, knowing that I had a longing for justice. I believe at that very moment she was truly proud of me. She got that look in her eyes, as she usually did when she was about to tell a story. She eased back in her rocking chair, took a deep breath and said, "Wayne, I got a story for you. It may be true. It may not. Regardless, it makes a good point."

I leaned forward and said, "Go grandmother, go!"

THE DAY VADA FRYE DIED

Hot September (In my words not hers)

Through the bloody red sky of the September twilight, aftermath of sixty-two rainless days that had spread like a fire in dry grass, the rumour was roaring through town. It was something about Miss Minnie Cooper and a Negro. Minnie had been attacked, insulted and frightened. None of them gathered in the barber shop on that Saturday evening where the ceiling fan whirred without freshening the stale air, actually knew exactly what had happened, as it was all supposition.

"Except it wasn't Will Mayes," said one barber, a man of middle age; a thin man with a mild face, who was shaving a client. "I know Will Mayes. He's a good nigger. And I know Miss Minnie Cooper, too."

"What do you know about her?" a second barber said.

"Who is she?" a client said. "A young girl?"

"No," the barber replied. "She's about forty. She ain't married. That's why I don't believe..."

"Believe, hell!" a hulking youth in a sweat-stained silk shirt said. "Won't you take a white woman's word before a nigger's?"

"I don't believe Will Mayes did it," the barber said. "I know Will Mayes."

"Maybe you know who did it, then. Maybe you already got him out of town, you damn nigger-lover."

"I don't believe anybody did anything. I don't believe anything happened. I leave it to you fellows if them ladies that get old without getting married don't have notions that a man can't... "

"Then you are a hell of a white man," another client said. He moved under the cloth.

The youth had sprung to his feet. "You don't?" he said. "Do you accuse a white woman of lying?"

The barber held the razor poised above the half-risen client. He did not look around.

"It's this weather," another said. "It's enough to make a man do anything. Even to her."

Nobody laughed. The barber said in his mild, stubborn tone: "I ain't accusing nobody of nothing. I just know and you fellows know how a woman that never..."

"You damn nigger-lover!" the youth said.

"Shut up, Butch," another said. "We'll get the facts in plenty of time to act."

"Who is? Who's getting them?" the youth said.

"Find out the truth first. I know Will Mayes," said the barber.

The client in one chair sat up. He looked at the speaker. "Do you claim that anything excuses a nigger attacking a white woman? Do you mean to tell me you are a white man and you'll stand for it? You better get up North where you came from. The South don't want your kind here."

"North what?" the second said. "I was born and raised in this here town."

"Well, by God!" the youth said. He looked about with a strained, baffled gaze, as if he was trying to remember what it was he wanted to say or to do. He drew his sleeve across his sweating face. "Damn if I'm going to let a white woman..."

"You tell them, Jack," another said.

The screen door crashed open. A man stood in the door, his feet apart and his heavy-set body poised easily. His white shirt was open at the throat; he wore a felt hat. His hot, bold glance swept the group. His name was McLendon. He had commanded troops at the front in France in World War I and had been decorated for valour. "Well," he said, "are you going to sit there and let a black son rape a white woman on the streets of Jefferson?"

Butch sprang up again. The silk of his shirt clung flat to his heavy shoulders. At each armpit was a dark half-moon from perspiration. "That's what I been telling them! That's what I..."

"Did it really happen?" a third said. "This ain't the first man scare she ever had. Wasn't there something about a man on the kitchen roof, watching her undress, about a year ago?"

"What?" the client said. "What's that?"

The barber had been slowly forcing him back into the chair; he arrested himself reclining, his head lifted, the barber still pressing him down. McLendon whirled about. "Happen? What the hell difference does it make? Are you going to let the black sons get away with it until one really does it?"

THE DAY VADA FRYE DIED

"That's what I'm telling them!" Butch shouted.

McLendon said; "no talking necessary at all. I've done my talking. Who's with me?" He poised on the balls of his feet, roving his gaze.

The barber held the client's face down, the razor poised. "Find out the facts first, boys. I know Willy Mayes. It wasn't him."

McLendon whirled upon the barber who did not look away. They stared at each other. The other barbers had ceased also above their prone clients.

"You mean to tell me," McLendon said, "that you'd take a nigger's word before a white woman's? Why, you damn nigger-loving..."

The third speaker rose and grasped McLendon's arm; he too had been a soldier. "Now, now. Let's figure this thing out. Who knows anything about what really happened?"

"Figure out hell!" McLendon said. "All that are with me get up from here. The ones that ain't..." He roved his gaze, dragging his sleeve across his face. Three men rose. Another rose and moved toward him. The remainder sat uncomfortable, not looking at one another. Then one by one they rose and joined him.

The sensible barber said, "Boys, don't do that. Will Mayes never done it. I know."

"Come on," McLendon said. From his hip pocket protruded the butt of a heavy automatic pistol.

They went out. The screen door crashed behind them, reverberant in the dead air. The barber wiped the razor carefully and swiftly, and put it away, and ran to the rear, and took his hat from the wall. "I'll be back as soon as I can," he said to the other barbers. "I can't let..."

He went out, running. The two other barbers followed him to the door and caught it on the rebound, leaning out and looking up the street after him. "What can he do?" the first said. The second one was saying "Jees Christ, Jees Christ" under his breath. "I pity Mayes the way McLendon is riled. You reckon he really done it to her?"

Minnie Cooper was thirty-eight or thirty-nine. She lived in a small frame house with her invalid mother and a thin, sallow, unflagging aunt, where each morning between ten and eleven she would appear on the porch in a lace-trimmed boudoir cap, to sit swinging in the porch swing until noon. After lunch she lay down for a while, until it began to cool off a bit. Then, in one of the three or four low cut silk dresses which she had each summer, she would go downtown to spend the afternoon in the stores with the other ladies, where they would handle the goods and haggle over the prices in cold, immediate voices, without any intention of buying. She was on the slender side of ordinary looking, with a bright, faintly haggard manner and dress. When she was young she had had a slender, nervous body and a sort of hard vivacity which had enabled her for a time to ride upon the crest of the town's social life as exemplified by the high school party and church social period of her contemporaries while still children enough to be un-class conscious. She was the last to realize that she was losing ground; that those among whom she had been a little brighter and louder flame than any other were beginning to learn snobbery. That was when her face began to wear that bright, haggard look. She watched the girls with whom she had grown up as they married and got homes and children. Then the town began to see her driving on Sunday afternoons with the cashier in the bank. He was a widower of about forty, smelling always faintly of the barber shop or of whisky. He owned a fancy automobile. Still he never popped the question.

It was twelve years now since she had been relegated into adultery by public opinion, and eight years since the cashier had gone to a Memphis bank, returning for one day each Christmas, which he spent at an annual bachelors' party at a hunting club on the river. From behind their curtains the neighbours would see the party pass, and during the over-the-way Christmas day visiting they would tell her about him, about how well he looked, and how they heard that he was prospering in the city, watching with bright, secret eyes her haggard, bright face. Usually by that hour there would be the scent of whisky on her breath. It was supplied her by a youth, a clerk at the soda fountain: "Sure; I buy it for the old gal."

THE DAY VADA FRYE DIED

The barber went swiftly up the street where the lights were just coming on and insects swirled about in the lifeless air. The day had died in a pall of dust; above the darkened square, shrouded by the spent dust, the sky was as clear as the inside of a brass bell. When he overtook them, McLendon and three others were getting into a car parked in an alley. McLendon stooped his thick head, peering out beneath the top, "Changed your mind, did you?" he said. "Damn good thing; by God, tomorrow when this town hears about how you talked tonight....."

"Now, now," the other ex-soldier said. "Bill's all right. Come on, Bill; jump in."

"Will Mayes never done it, boys," the barber said. "If anybody done it. Why, you all know well as I do there ain't any town where they got better niggers than us. And you know how a lady will kind of think things about men when there ain't any reason to, and Miss Minnie anyway..."

"Sure, sure," the soldier said. "We're just going to talk to him a little; that's all. Just a little talking."

"Talk hell!" another said. "When we're through with the..."

"Shut up, for God's sake!" the soldier said. "Do you want everybody in town..."

"Tell them, by God!" McLendon said. "Tell every one of the sons that'll let a white woman..."

THE DAY VADA FRYE DIED

"Let's go; let's go: here's the other car." The second car slid squealing out of a cloud of dust at the alley mouth. McLendon started his car and took the lead. Dust lay like fog in the street. They drove on out of town past the ice plant, where Mayes was night watchman.

"Better stop here, hadn't we?" the soldier said.

McLendon did not reply. He hurled the car up and slammed to a stop, the headlights glaring on the blank wall.

"Listen here, boys," said the barber, who had decided to go along only hoping he could calm them down. "If he's here, don't that prove he never done it? Don't it? If it was him, he would run. Don't you see he would?"

The second car came up and stopped. McLendon got out.

"Listen, boys," the barber said. "Cut the lights off!"

The breathless dark rushed down. There was no sound in it save their lungs as they sought air in the parched dust in which for two months they had lived; then the diminishing crunch of McLendon's stomping feet, and a moment later McLendon's voice: "Will!... Will!" Below the east, the haemorrhaging of the moon increased. It heaved above the ridge, silvering the air and the dust, so that they seemed to breathe in a bowl of molten lead. There was no sound of night birds or insects, no sound save their breathing and a faint ticking of contracting metal about the cars. Where their bodies touched one another they seemed to sweat dryly, for no more moisture came. "Christ!" a voice said; "let's get out of here." But they didn't move until vague noises began to grow out of the darkness ahead; then they got out and waited tensely in the breathless dark. There was another sound: a blow, a hissing expulsion of breath and McLendon cursing in deep undertones. They stood a moment longer, and then they ran forward. They ran in a stumbling clump, as though they were fleeing something.

"Kill him, kill the son," a voice whispered. McLendon flung them back. "Not here," he said. "Get him into the car."

"Kill him, kill the black son..." the voice murmured as they dragged Mayes to the car. The barber had waited beside the car. He could feel himself sweating, and he knew he was going to be sick at his stomach.

"What is it?" the Negro said. "I ain't done nothing."

Someone produced handcuffs. They worked busily about the Negro as though he were a post, quiet, intent, getting in one another's way. He submitted to the handcuffs, looking swiftly and constantly from dim face to dim face. "Who's here? Why is ya'lls doing this?" he said, leaning to peer into the faces until they could feel his breath and smell his sweaty reek. He spoke a name or two. "What you all say I done, Mr. John?"

McLendon jerked the car door open. "Get in!" he said.

The Negro did not move. "What you all going to do with me, Mr. John? I ain't done nothing. White folks, I ain't done nothing: I swear 'fore God." He called another name.

"Get in!" McLendon said as he struck the Negro. The others expelled their breath in a dry hissing and struck him with random blows and he whirled and cursed them, and swept his manacled hands across their faces and slashed the barber upon the mouth, and the barber struck him also. "Get him in there," McLendon said.

They pushed at him. He ceased struggling and got into the car willingly and sat quietly as the others took their places. He sat fearfully between the barber and the soldier, drawing his limbs in so as not to touch them, his eyes going swiftly and constantly from face to face. The car moved on.

The barber nursed his mouth with his handkerchief. "What's the matter?" the soldier said.

"Nothing," the barber replied.

They regained the highroad and turned away from town. The second car dropped back out of the dust. They went on, gaining speed; the final fringe of houses dropped behind. "Damn, he stinks!" the soldier said.

"We'll fix that," one in the front beside McLendon said.

THE DAY VADA FRYE DIED

The barber leaned suddenly forward and touched McLendon's arm. "Let me out, John," he said.

"Jump out, nigger-lover, cause we ain't stopping," McLendon said without turning his head. He drove swiftly. Behind them the source-less lights of the second car glared in the dust. Presently McLendon turned into a narrow road. It was rutted with disuse. It led back to an abandoned brick kiln, a series of reddish mounds and weed and vine-choked vats without bottom.

"John," the barber said.

"Jump out, then," McLendon said, hurling the car along the ruts.

Beside the barber the Negro spoke: "Please fellas, please."

The barber sat forward. The narrow tunnel of the road rushed up and past. Their motion was like an extinct furnace blast: cooler, but utterly dead. The car bounded from rut to rut.

"Mr. Henry," the Negro said as the barber began to tug furiously at the door.

"Look out, there!" the soldier said, but the barber had already kicked the door open and rolled out onto the ground. The soldier leaned across the Negro and grasped at him, as he jumped out, too, rolling into a corn field.

The impetus hurled the barber crashing through dust-sheathed weeds, into the ditch. Dust puffed about him, and in a thin, vicious crackling of sapless stems he laid choking and retching until the second car passed and died away. Then he rose and limped on until he reached the highroad and turned toward town, brushing at his clothes with his hands. The moon was higher, riding high and clear of the dust at last, and after a while the town began to glare beneath the dust. He went on, limping. Presently he heard cars and the glow of them grew in the dust behind him and he left the road and crouched again in the weeds until they passed. McLendon's car came last.

The perpetrators tore on, fearful now that the Negro would get back to town and find the sheriff. The dust swallowed them; the glare and the sound died away. Meanwhile, the barber climbed back onto the road and limped on toward town, not realizing that off the road in the cornfields was Mayes also making his way to town.

As Minnie Cooper dressed for supper on that Saturday evening, her own flesh felt like fever. Her hands trembled among the buttons, and her eyes had a feverish look, and her hair swirled crisp and crackling under the comb. While she was still dressing the friends called for her and sat while she donned her sheerest under things and stockings and a new dress. "Do you feel strong enough to go out?" they said, their eyes bright with a dark glitter. "When you have had time to get over the shock, you must tell us what happened. What he said and did; everything."

THE DAY VADA FRYE DIED

In the leafed darkness, as they walked toward the square, she began to breathe deeply, something like a swimmer preparing to dive, until she ceased trembling. The four of them walked slowly because of the terrible heat and out of solicitude for her. But as they neared the square she began to tremble again, walking with her head up, her hands clenched at her sides. They entered the square, she in the center of the group, fragile in her fresh dress. She was trembling worse. She walked slower and slower, as children ate ice cream. Her head was held up and her eyes bright in the haggard banner of her face. As they passed the hotel, the murmuring voices could be heard. "That's the one: see? The one in pink in the middle. Is that her? What did they do with the nigger? Did they? Sure. He's all right. All right, is he? Sure. He went on a little trip."

Then they moved past the drug store, where even the young men lounging in the doorway tipped their hats and followed with their eyes the motion of Minnie's hips and legs when she passed. They went on, passing the lifted hats of the gentlemen, the suddenly ceased voices, deferent, protective. "Do you see?" the friends said. Their voices sounded like long, hovering sighs of hissing exultation. "There's not a Negro on the square. Not one."

The group of women reached the picture show. It was like a miniature fairyland with its lighted lobby and coloured lithographs of life caught in its terrible and beautiful mutations. Minnie's lips began to tingle. In the dark, when the picture began, it would be all right; she could hold back the laughing so it would not waste away so fast and so soon. So she hurried on before the turning faces, the undertones of low astonishment, and they took their accustomed places where she could see the aisle against the silver glare and the young men and girls coming in two and two against it. The lights flicked away; the screen glowed silver, and soon life began to unfold, beautiful and passionate and sad, while still the young men and girls entered, scented and sibilant in the half dark, their paired backs in silhouette delicate and sleek, their slim, quick bodies awkward, divinely young, while beyond them the silver dream accumulated, inevitably on and on.

Minnie began to babble. In trying to suppress it, she made more noise than ever. Heads began to turn. Still babbling incoherently, her friends raised her and led her out, and she stood at the curb, babbling gibberish on a high, sustained note, until the taxi came up and they helped her in. They went home with her, removed her dress and the sheer under things and the stockings, and put her to bed, and cracked ice for her temples and sent for the doctor.

She was frantic, so they ministered to her without uttering a word, renewing the ice and fanning her. While the ice was fresh and cold she stopped muttering and lay still for a time, moaning only a little. But soon the gibberish welled again and her voice rose screaming. "Shhhhhhhhhhh! Shhhhhhhhhhhhhh!" they said, freshening the icepack, smoothing her hair, as they uttered "poor girl!" Then to one another: "Do you suppose anything really happened?" Their eyes were darkly aglitter, secret and passionate.

"Shhhhhhhhhh! Poor girl! Poor Minnie!"

It was midnight when McLendon drove up to his neat new house. It was trim and fresh as a birdcage and almost as small, with its clean, green-and-white paint. He locked the car and mounted the porch and entered. His wife rose from a chair beside the reading lamp. McLendon stopped and stared at her until she looked down. "Look at that clock," he said, lifting his arm, pointing. She stood before him, her face lowered, a magazine in her hands. Her face was pale, strained, and weary-looking. "Haven't I told you about sitting up like this, waiting to see when I come in?"

"John," she said, as she laid the magazine she was holding down.

Poised on the balls of his feet, he glared at her with his hot eyes, his sweating face. "Didn't I tell you?"

He went toward her. She looked up then. He caught her shoulder. She stood passive, looking at him. "Don't, John. I couldn't sleep. The heat - something. Please, John. You're hurting me."

THE DAY VADA FRYE DIED

"Didn't I tell you?" He released her and half struck, half flung her across the chair, and she lay there and watched him quietly as he left the room. He went on through the house, ripping off his shirt, and on the dark, screened porch at the rear he stood and mopped his head and shoulders with the shirt and flung it away. He went into the bedroom, took the pistol from his hip and laid it on the table beside the bed and sat on the bed and removed his shoes, rose and slipped his trousers off. He looked outside, fearful that the truth might be found out. There was no movement, no sound, not even an insect. The dark world seemed to lie stricken beneath the cold moon and the lidless stars.

His wife had gotten to her feet, moved to the bedroom archway, stood looking down at him and said, "I know what you did!"

He glared up at her and shouted, "You'd better keep your mouth shut."

Meanwhile, Mayes had fallen among the corn. He was breathing heavily, fearful that he would be found. His wrists were hurting from the handcuffs which had been put on too tightly. He looked up at the starry night sky and started to cry. Being a person of colour in the south was a taxing experience and there was no end to the misery one had to endure just to stay alive. What was the use? He took a deep breath and his heart stopped. His struggles were over.

Back at Minnie's house, she was alone now, as all her companions had departed. She started crying, terribly fearful of the man who had attacked her. The man had told her to make up a story about a Negro attacking her, and if she didn't he would see that she suffered dire consequences.

There were several victims of the evil of prejudice that night. First was poor old Mayes, who had done no wrong. There was Minnie who had been attacked and was fearful of revealing who her real attacker was; and thereby, perpetrated a lie at the behest of her attacker. There was Mrs. McLendon who lived in fear of her abusive husband, and feared revealing the truth because of his wrath. Ultimately there was John McLendon, who lived in a patricidal fairyland where men were superior to women, but above all where white men were superior to people of colour and could never be made to pay for any crimes against people of colour. He had attacked Minnie, and he had indirectly caused the death of Mayes in an attempt to cover up his crime. Prejudice my dear Wayne is a burden that confuses the past, threatens the future and renders hope impossible.

- - -

I looked at my grandmother as she rocked away and said, "Emmett Till is a victim of evil grandmother. We have to fight that evil."

She replied, "We'll do our best, but taking a stand against prejudice in the society in which we live can get you killed. So be careful."

THE DAY VADA FRYE DIED

I realized at that very moment that my grandmother had tried valiantly to fight the norms for the society in which she was reared, a society that clung to a glamorized past that made heroes out of people who fought to keep others in bondage. I realized the dilemma faced by so many, as did my grandmother. Conform or be ostracized, which is what people in her story did. It was something I had done and would do in the future, much to my shame. It is a shame I have carried with me to this very day, the shame of too often not taking a stand against the evil of prejudice.

I grew up at a time of institutionalized racism in the southern USA. I think what I understand now about racism is just how quiet it was. Being white, when I was young I did not really recognize racism, and when I became old enough to recognize it I was, for many years, just accepting of it, because I had been propagandized into believing it was okay. People lived in segregated areas of the small town of Asheboro, North Carolina, and there were separate schools: consequently, my primary association with African-Americans was simply passing them on the streets. Of course, I never saw any of them in restaurants, when I would go out to eat with my family, because they were not allowed in the seating area. They could cook the food in the kitchen of the restaurant, but if they wanted to eat food from the restaurant they had to have it handed to them out the back door. That is just the way it was, and when I was young I accepted it without reservation, but thanks to my grandmother, who had also been conditioned to accept it, because of her natural inclination to treat all people equally, I saw that she and my grandfather questioned the validity of a system where the term "all men are equal" was ballyhooed across a nation that was absolutely hypocritical in its actual application, because particularly in the southern USA, about 40% of the population was considered unworthy of equality.

I had a questioning nature as did my grandmother, but it is difficult to take a stand when all about you are opposed to justice. However, my grandmother and I both loved the Rudyard Kipling poem, *If*.

If you can keep your head when all about you
Are losing theirs and blaming it on you,
If you can trust yourself when all men doubt you,
But make allowance for their doubting too;
If you can wait and not be tired by waiting,
Or being lied about, don't deal in lies,
Or being hated, don't give way to hating,
And yet don't look too good, nor talk too wise:

If you can dream & not make dreams your master;
If you can think—and not make thoughts your aim;
If you can meet with Triumph and Disaster
And treat those two impostors just the same;

THE DAY VADA FRYE DIED

If you can bear to hear the truth you've spoken
Twisted by knaves to make a trap for fools,
Or watch the things you gave your life to, broken,
And stoop and build 'em up with worn-out tools:

If you can make one heap of all your winnings
And risk it on one turn of pitch-and-toss,
And lose, and start again at your beginnings,
And never breathe a word about your loss;
If you can force your heart and nerve and sinew
To serve your turn long after they are gone,
And so hold on when there is nothing in you
Except the Will which says to them: 'Hold on!'

If you can talk with crowds and keep your virtue,
Or walk with Kings—nor lose the common touch,
If neither foes nor loving friends can hurt you,
If all men count with you, but none too much;
If you can fill the unforgiving minute
With sixty seconds' worth of distance run,
Yours is the Earth and everything that's in it,
And—which is more—you'll be a Man, my son!

When I read her the poem, we spent hours going over its meaning and discussing each line. Her lack of education never dulled her urge to learn, because she told me that if you ever stopped learning you might as well stop breathing. This was never more evident than when I crossed a barrier in the small town where we lived that was never crossed, because it could destroy a person. I was fifteen years old and had renewed a friendship from my childhood with an African American young man who lived in the section of town that was called "Nigger Hill." In fact, I had always referred to the section of town where African-Americans lived by that despicable name, because that is what it was called by all the whites in town. I was either too young, too idiotic or too brainwashed to realize its abhorrent nature as a derogatory term.

My friend, Colin Loudermilk, the African American I had met when I was very young and we had played together when his father did some work for my grandmother, would become one of my best friends. We had developed great rapport, but even though his father had invited me over to their home, I had never gone because of where it was. Many years passed and one day his father was doing some work at a home near where my grandmother lived and he let me know that Colin was still wondering why I never showed up for a visit. I was ashamed to tell him why, and at fifteen I decided that decorum be damned, I was going over to see him. I went over many times and even hung out on "the hill" almost weekly. Colin introduced me to an African American girl, and that would be the crowning catalyst in developing my realization of the evil of prejudice. There is nothing like a flaming romance to breach the barriers between races, and my torrid affair would eventually lead to me actually introducing the young lady in question to my grandmother, because I felt it incumbent upon me to always get her seal of approval on all my girlfriends.

She was not appalled that I was having a romance with an African American girl, but she warned me to be careful and not to let my parents know about it. She promised not to tell, and much to my delight, she had positive things to say about how nice the girl was. I rarely visited my grandmother's with her, because much to my shame today, I was afraid being seen with her would lead to negative reactions from my white friends. We did all our romancing on the hill, mostly at her home and at a nearby store with a dining porch. One day she left town, because her mother got a job in Kansas City, and I would never see her again. My grandmother consoled me, saying that there would be many loves in my life, and that each one would remain in my heart a lifetime, because love was like water – you needed it to survive.

How I wish I would have had the courage at the time to walk down the streets of Asheboro, North Carolina holding her hand, defying convention for the sake of love!

THE DAY VADA FRYE DIED

Chapter 8
It is Over - It is Done

*Farewell to thee! But not farewell
To all my fondest thoughts of thee.
Within my heart they still shall dwell,
And they shall cheer and comfort me.*

*O, thou are beautiful and full of grace!
If thou had never met mine eye,
If I had not dreamed a living face,
Could I but love you with a sigh.*

*If I may ne'er behold again
That form and face so dear to me,
Nor hear thy voice, still would I fain,
And reserve for eternity thy memory.*

J. Wayne Frye   125

THE DAY VADA FRYE DIED

That voice, the magic of whose tone
Can wake an echo in my breast,
Creating feelings that, alone,
Can make my spirit blest.

That laughing eye whose sunny beam
My memory would not cherish less;
And oh, that smile whose joyous gleam
No mortal language can express.

Adieu, but let me cherish, still,
The hope with which I cannot part.
I am forever wounded, and know chill,
But still your love lingers in my heart.

And who can tell when you'll draw your last,
Without you how will I deal with my fears,
And bid in the future to pay for the past,
Replacing joy for anguish and smiles for tears.

Still I pleaded, "Please don't leave me. Please don't leave me." However, I was beginning to realize my pleas were having no lasting effect. Had she truly just been waiting for me to return from my trip to die, and were my pleas just somehow making her linger when she desperately wanted to go?

In death, just like in life, sometimes there is a reaching out, one soul stretching across the darkness toward another. It was not a scary feeling, nothing about my grandmother was ever scary, but it was a lonely feeling as I felt

J. Wayne Frye

lost in the blackness of despair. I was seething with pain, but I was beginning to realize my selfishness. I simply wanted her to stay, because I needed her so desperately.

Death was a dark cloak glad skeletal figure with a scythe waiting in the hospital corridor to claim the person I loved most in the world. My friend, Mickey Spillane, had often used that image of death standing with a scythe in his books, and once when we were having a discussion on the dock outside his Merrill's Inlet home he had said to me: "Life is pleasant. Death is peaceful. It's the transition from one to the other that is hell."

I was experiencing that hell as I looked upon my beloved grandmother lying on that bed. But she was still breathing, so there was life. I recalled what Dylan Thomas had said about dying, "Do not go gentle into that good night. Old age should burn and rave at close of day. Rage, rage against the dying of the light." Yes, please I thought to myself, please my dear grandmother rage against the dying of the light, not for yourself but for me.

As alluded to earlier, Americans are afraid of the word death. They came up with the ridiculous term "passing." I suppose that is just another part of the religious propaganda that is spewed out from the pulpits of manipulation where God's anointed dispensers of wisdom prepare people for the glory of heaven, a place where the streets are paved with gold. Of course they would be paved with gold, because Americans worship money almost as much as they worship God, maybe more. Death is just a form of passing from one life to another according to Christians. What about those going to hell? I suppose they are also "passing," not dying, because they will pass into eternity in the bowels of the earth where the raging fires of hell will consume them as little red men with horns and pitchforks keep prodding them into the fire.

I got a kick out of my father who said that he knew he was going to hell, but it was alright, because he always wanted to be where the crowd was.

My grandfather often said that if a lot of the Christians he knew were going to heaven that eternity with them would actually be hell. He was a true scholar of the Bible, despite having no belief of what he called fairy tales in a book filled with evil like telling a father to sell his daughter to the highest bidder or encouraging the killing of a rebellious son. I remember one Saturday night as we sat on the porch swing watching cars whiz by on the highway below he discussed with my grandmother the idea that Jesus was not a white person. He said, in exactness, "First, Jesus Christ was a mixed-blood Saviour of mankind, not a pure-blooded Jew. Matthew's genealogy of Christ (Matthew 1:1-17) interestingly highlights five women: Tamar, who seduced her father-in-law in order

THE DAY VADA FRYE DIED

to carry on the line of Er (Genesis 38); Rahab
the prostitute; Ruth the Moabite; Uriah's wife,
Bathsheba; and Mary, Jesus' mother. Only Mary
was definitively Jewish. Rahab was a Canaanite,
and Tamar was possibly one too. Ruth was a
Moabite, and Bathsheba, being the wife of Uriah
the Hittite, was likely a Hittite herself. Yet all of
them were ancestors of Jesus the Messiah. So,
when you go into church and see that white
faced Jesus, you are looking at an image that
just ain't him, ain't no where close to being him,
because he was a mixed race person. Now, I am
saying this as a result of what I have studied.
You can read it yourself if you want. Of course, I
don't believe none of that fairy tale
gobbledygook, but those that do want to follow
the Bible, and if they 'un want to follow it they
better damn well know that the man named
Jesus ain't no 100% white man. That'll sure not
set well with them folks always preaching
about separation of races."

My grandmother looked over at me and said,
"Looks like the Reverend Dixon Frye has
delivered another sermon tonight." We all had a
good laugh.

In 1967, my grandfather had been dead for
ten years, and he and I were not as close as I
was to my grandmother, but as time moved on I
began to realize what high esteem I had for
him. Now, my grandmother would be gone, too.
I feared for myself, feared that I would no
longer have the confidant I needed to survive.

THE DAY VADA FRYE DIED

Each hour I looked forlornly down at her, looked down as life was escaping from her body. The ghostly hands of a fitful wind began to stir outside. I could smell the perfume of lilies stealing in from under the slightly open window. Far off in the distance I could see dogwood trees, standing tall against the silver dawn-lit sky like the twin spires of some cathedral. Just between them hung a dimly-lit half moon. All this seemed to comfort me and ease the stress of my vigil.

Death is the great equalizer of human beings. Death is the boundary that we need to measure the precious texture of our lives. All people owe the debt of death. For those left behind like I feared to be, death paints everything a different shade of remorse, but I knew I would have no remorse, because she always knew I loved her above everyone else. The bond we shared was unbreakable, even with death.

I got up from my chair, walked to the door, slowly opened it and turned to my right, looking down the hall. I could not see it but could sense it. He was there in the shadows, waiting with that damn scythe in his hands. His secret was that though he was death, and supposedly beyond all wanting that he actually wanted something that my grandmother and I shared. He yearned and mourned and raged in his heart for something that only mortals can obtain. And what was it that he wanted and wept in his heart for? A genuine love of his own as deep and abiding as the love my grandmother and I shared. He wanted a person who would comfort his heart when it broke from the sadness of his terrible errands of death, who would weep with him when he carried dead children, the dead of any age in his arms, someone who could weep with him over the misery of his job. He was there waiting to take my grandmother. I thought for a second would he take me too, because I was not sure I could go on living without her.

At that moment, I walked back into my grandmother's room, and noticed her breathing was less laboured. There was a new rhythm to the intensity of her breathing, a peaceful calm as her chest gently rose and lowered. I eased into the bedside chair and reached out to, as I had done so many times before, hold her hand. It was warmer than usual. Staring down at her, I reflected on one of my grandmother's stories, one that epitomized the true power of love, and how even death cannot assuage its intensity. It was not a story of grandmother-grandson love, but of a romantic love between a man and a woman. It was one of those grand southern stories which glossed over the evil of fighting to defend slavery, but still offered a true glimpse of how powerful love can be in the grand scheme of things. It was one of her best stories, and it was a perfect example of how time does not diminish love even after death. It was a perfect time to remember a perfect story.

THE DAY VADA FRYE DIED

Grey Death (Retold in my words, not hers.)

When Miss Diane Greer died, the whole town went to her funeral: the men through a sort of respectful affection for a fallen monument, the women mostly out of curiosity to see the inside of her house, which no one save an old man-servant-combined gardener and cook had seen in so many years.

It was a big, squared frame house that had once been white, decorated with cupolas and spires and scrolled balconies set on what had once been the town's most select street. But garages and cotton gins had encroached and obliterated even the august names of that neighborhood; only Miss Diane's house was left, lifting its stubborn and coquettish decay above the cotton wagons and the gasoline pumps. It was an eyesore among eyesores. And now Miss Diane had gone to join the representatives of those august names where they lay in the cedar-bemused cemetery among the ranked and anonymous graves of Union and Confederate soldiers who fell at the Battle of Jefferson County.

Alive, Miss Diane had been a tradition, a duty, and a care; a sort of hereditary obligation upon the town, dating from who knew when. The woman came from a wealthy family, but the wealth had dissipated over the years as had the family. Not that Miss Diane would have accepted charity. The town mayor had invented an involved tale to the effect that Miss Diane's father had lent money to the town, which the town, as a matter of business, preferred to repay by helping Miss Diane survive all through the years when only she was left from the once prominent family. It was not really a believable story, but out of affection for Miss Diane the townsfolk went along with it.

When the next generation, with its more modern ideas, became mayors and aldermen, this arrangement created some little dissatisfaction. On the first of the year they mailed her a tax notice. February came, and there was no reply. They wrote her a formal letter, asking her to call at the sheriff's office at her convenience. A week later the mayor wrote her himself, offering to call or to send his car for her, and received in reply a note on paper of an archaic shape, in a thin, flowing calligraphy in faded ink, to the effect that she no longer went out at all. The tax notice was also enclosed, without comment.

They called a special meeting of the Board of Aldermen. A deputy waited upon her, knocked at the door through which no visitor had passed since so many years that people had lost count. They were admitted by the old African-American man who had served as her valet, gardener, etc. for years into a dim hall below a stairway. It smelled of dust and disuse. The African-American led them into the parlour. It was furnished in heavy, leather-covered furniture. When the servant opened the blinds of one window, they could see that the leather was cracked; and when they sat down a faint dust rose sluggishly about their thighs, spinning with slow motes in the single sun-ray. On a tarnished gilt easel before the fireplace stood a crayon portrait of Miss Diane's father.

They rose when she entered, a small, fat woman in black, with a thin gold chain descending to her waist and vanishing into her belt, leaning on an ebony cane with a tarnished gold knob. Her skeleton was small and spare; perhaps that was why what would have been merely plumpness in another was obesity in her. She looked bloated, like a body long submerged in motionless water and of pallid hue. Her eyes, lost in the fatty ridges of her face, looked like two small pieces of coal pressed into a lump of dough as they moved from one face to another while the visitors stated their errand.

She just stood in the doorway and listened quietly until one of the spokesman came to a stumbling halt. Then they could hear the unseen watch ticking at the end of the gold chain in her pocket.

Her voice was dry and cold. "I have no taxes in Jefferson. The former mayor explained it to me. Yes, no taxes owing to my father's benevolence to the town so many years ago when he lent money that was never repaid. Perhaps one of you can gain access to the city records and satisfy yourselves."

THE DAY VADA FRYE DIED

"But we have. We are the city authorities, Miss Diane. Didn't you get a notice from the sheriff, signed by him?"

"I received a paper, yes," Miss Diane said. "I tell you I have no taxes."

"But there is nothing on the books to show that you see. We must go by the books."

"See Mayor Donnelly. I have no taxes."

"But, Ma'am, Mayor Donnelly has been dead for years now."

"Poppycock! I have no taxes!"

The servant suddenly appeared and Miss Diane barked, "Show these gentlemen out."

So she vanquished them, just as she had vanquished their fathers thirty years before.

That previous banishment was two years after her father's death and a short time after her sweetheart, the one people believed she would marry had deserted her. After her father's death she went out very little; after her sweetheart went away, people hardly saw her at all. A few of the ladies had the temerity to call, but were not received, and the only sign of life about the place was the servant, a young man then, going in and out with a market basket. Of course he was far beyond middle age now, and, no doubt, unable to keep the house up, though he tried. In fact, there were putrid smells emanating from the house, smells so putrid that people said laughingly that she must have dead bodies in there, rotting, as it were, and fouling the air all around the estate.

THE DAY VADA FRYE DIED

A neighbour woman complained to the mayor about the horrible smell.

"But what will you have me do about it, madam?" he said.

"Why, send her word to stop it," the woman said. "Isn't there a law?"

"I'm sure that won't be necessary," the mayor said. "It's probably just a snake or a rat that servant of hers killed in the yard. I'll speak to him about it."

The next day he received two more complaints, one from a man who came in diffident deprecation. "We really must do something about it, Mayor. I'd be the last one in the world to bother Miss Diane, but we've got to do something."

That night the Board of Aldermen met and they decided to send her word to clean the place up. She did not reply, so the next night, after midnight, four men crossed Miss Diane's lawn and slunk about the house like burglars, sniffing along the base of the brickwork and at the cellar openings. They broke open the cellar door and sprinkled lime there, and in all the outbuildings. As they re-crossed the lawn, a window that had been dark was lighted and Miss Diane sat in front of it, the light behind her, and her upright torso motionless as that of an idol. They crept quietly across the lawn and into the shadow of the darkness that lined the street. After a week or two, the smell went away.

J. Wayne Frye

THE DAY VADA FRYE DIED

That was when people had begun to feel really sorry for her. People in the town, remembering how Diane's mother, her great-aunt and the few other living family members believed that the family was somehow exalted. None of the young men of the town were quite good enough for Miss Diane as a result. So when she got to be thirty and was still single, the people in the town were actually pleased; even with a propensity for insanity in the family she wouldn't have turned down all of her chances if they had really materialized. It was as if Diane was paying the price for her family's eccentricity.

When all of her family died, including her father, it got about that the house was all that was left to her; and in a way, people were glad. At last they assumed being left alone, and a pauper, she had to become humanized. Now she too would know the agony of normal people who had to struggle day-to-day in order to survive.

The day after her father's death all the ladies prepared to call at the house and offer condolence and aid. Miss Diane met them at the door, dressed as usual with no trace of grief on her face. She told them that her father was not dead. She did that for three days, with the ministers calling on her, and the doctors, trying to persuade her to let them dispose of the body. Just as they were about to go to law she broke down, and they buried her father quickly.

THE DAY VADA FRYE DIED

The townsfolk remembered all the young men her father had driven away, and they knew that with no family left, she would actually miss the man who had caused that calamity.

She was sick for a long time. When the people saw her again, her hair was cut short, making her look like a girl, with a vague resemblance to those angels in church windows, sort of tragic and serene.

The town had just let the contracts for paving the sidewalks, and in the summer after her father's death they began the work. The construction company came with workers and mules and machinery, and a foreman named Homer Barron, a Yankee who was a big, dark, ready man, with a big voice and eyes lighter than his face. The little boys would follow in groups to hear him cuss the workers, and the workers singing in time to the rise and fall of picks. Pretty soon he knew everybody in town. Whenever you heard a lot of laughing anywhere about the square, Homer Barron would be in the center of the group. Presently they began to see him and Miss Diane on Sunday afternoons driving in the yellow-wheeled buggy and the matched team of horses from the livery stable.

At first they were glad that Miss Diane would have an interest, because the ladies all said, "Of course Miss Diane would not think seriously of a Northerner, a day labourer." And there were still others, older people, who said that even grief could not cause a real lady to forget her stature in life to court someone of such low breeding.

Soon the old people started whispering, "Poor Diane." Oh, but whispering did not seem to bother her. In fact, she carried her head high almost as if she had regained a sense of importance. She was in love. It was as if she demanded more than ever the recognition of her dignity as the last of her clan; as if she had wanted that touch of earthiness to reaffirm her imperviousness.

After the road work was finished, Homer actually moved into her house and the whole town thought the situation was absolutely scandalous. Still, neither of the lovers cared.

After living together for a few months the two went to the jewellery store and purchased rings. The minister from the town's church was summoned to their house and the two were married. They lived, apparently happily, in that old house, never venturing out. Rather, they sent the servant out to attend to their needs.

Then after about three months of marriage, the town doctor was summoned. Homer had contracted pneumonia. Within a few days, he was dead.

The townsfolk rushed to console the recluse, Diane. She was distraught beyond description, but when they offered to help arrange his funeral she dismissed them, saying she would send the body to a crematory in the city.

THE DAY VADA FRYE DIED

"She will kill herself," proclaimed many.

Yet, she did not. She only retreated into solitude, and the servant continued serving her needs and buying whatever she needed from town going in and out with the market basket, but the front door remained closed to the world. Now and then she could be seen at the upstairs window for a moment, as the men did that night when they semi-raided her house because of the smell, but for year upon year she did not appear on the streets. Then this was to be expected; as if that quality of her father which had thwarted her lust for happiness so many times had been too virulent and too furious to die when he did. No, she was his daughter and had adopted his ways.

The image seen in the window changed over the years as she aged. She grew obese and her hair was turning grey. During the next few years it grew greyer and greyer until it attained an even pepper-and-salt iron-grey, when it ceased turning. Up to the day of her death at seventy-four it was still that vigorous iron-grey.

From that time on her front door remained closed. When the town got free postal delivery, Miss Diane alone refused to let them fasten the metal numbers above her door and attach a mailbox to it. She would not listen to them.

Daily, monthly, yearly people watched the servant grow greyer and more stooped, going in and out with the market basket. Each December she was sent her a tax notice, which would be returned by the post office a week later, unclaimed. Now and then she could be seen in one of the downstairs windows. She had evidently shut up the top floor of the house, although a light could be seen up there every night, a light that peaked out from the pulled curtains that always remained closed. Thus she passed on from one generation to next inescapable, impervious and perverse interest until she died exactly forty years after the love of her life had died. She fell ill in the house filled with dust and shadows, with only a doddering servant to wait on her. No doctors were called. She just went to her upstairs bedroom, where she laid waiting for the inevitable.

Upon her death, per her instructions, the servant moved her body to the downstairs sofa. It was there where the coroner found her body and removed it from the house for the first time in forty years.

The servant met the first of the ladies at the front door and let them in, with their hushed, sibilant voices and their quick, curious glances, and then he disappeared. He walked right through the house and out the back and was never seen again.

The funeral was on the second day after her death, with the town coming to look at Miss Diane beneath a mass of bought flowers, with the crayon face of her father musing profoundly above the fireplace and the ladies sibilant and macabre; and many old men sat on the porch and the lawn, talking of Miss Diane, believing that they had danced with her and courted her perhaps, confusing time with its mathematical progression, as the old do, to whom all the past is not a diminishing road but, instead, a huge meadow which no winter ever quite touches, divided from them now by the narrow bottleneck of the most recent decade of years.

Already all knew that there was one room in that region above stairs which no one had seen in forty years, and which would have to be forced open, because it had been locked by the servant as ordered by Miss Diane, and the key could not be found. They waited until Miss Diane was decently in the ground before they opened it.

The violence of breaking down the door seemed to fill the room with pervading dust. A thin, acrid pall as of the tomb seemed to lie everywhere upon this room decked and furnished as if for a bridal den. The room had valance curtains of faded rose colour. Upon the rose-shaded lights, upon the dressing table, upon the delicate array of crystal and the man's toilet things was much tarnished silver, silver so tarnished that the monogram was obscured, showing a loving placement from someone who truly valued the manliness of the surroundings. There was affectionate grandeur to the room, a grandeur that permeated with the love of one person for another. Yet, there was a sadness which seemed to overwhelm the intruders.

THE DAY VADA FRYE DIED

Among the things in the room, on a velvet chair in the far corner lay a collar and tie, as if they had just been removed, which, when lifted, left upon the surface a pale crescent in the dust that had accumulated there over the years. Upon another chair hung a suit, carefully folded; beneath it the two mute shoes and discarded socks. The man himself lay in the bed.

For a long while the people just stood there, looking down at the profound and fleshless grin on the deteriorated corpse of a man. The body was slightly turned apparently in the attitude of an embrace, but now the long sleep that outlasts love, that conquers even the grimace of love, had descended upon him. What was left of him, rotted beneath what was left of the nightshirt, had become inextricable from the bed in which he lay; and upon him and upon the pillow beside him lay that even coating of the patient and biding dust.

Then they noticed that in the second pillow was the indentation of a head. One of them lifted something from it, and leaning forward, that faint and invisible dust dry and acrid smell penetrated their nostrils as they saw a long strand of iron-grey hair.

- - -

Oh, how I had loved that story at that time in my life. Maybe loved it more than any of her stories, because it was so apropos at the very moment I sat by my grandmother's bedside, realizing just how much love I had for her, realizing that our connection was not temporary but for all time. I had been pleading with the words, "Please don't leave me," but after reflecting on that story, I realized how selfish I was being. I had made the situation all about me, not about her. Sometimes love is letting go. I realized that death ends a life but not a relationship. I remembered reading somewhere that you should not think of it as dying, but rather leaving early to avoid the rush, because all of us must catch that train out of the station one day. She had been waiting to catch the train, but could not leave until I told her goodbye.

I leaned over and whispered in her ear, "It's alright grandmother if you want to go."

Those must have been the words she was waiting for all that time, because almost instantly she took one last deep breathe, and within her chest there came a gurgling sound, a sound that said to me – "It is over. It is done."

Epilogue
The Day Vada Frye Died

You can shed tears
that she is gone,
or you can smile
because she has lived.

You can close eyes,
hoping she'll come back,
or you can open your eyes,
and see all that she has left.

Your heart can be empty,
because you can't see her,
or you can be full of the love
that you two shared.

J. Wayne Frye

THE DAY VADA FRYE DIED

You can turn your back on tomorrow
and live in yesterday,
or you can be happy for tomorrow
because of yesterday.

You can remember her,
and only that she is gone,
or you can cherish her memory
and let it live on.

You can cry and close your mind,
be empty and turn your back,
or you can do what she would want:
smile, open your eyes, love and go on.

People in the real world always say, when something terrible happens that the sadness and loss and aching pain of the heart will lessen as time passes, but it isn't true. Sorrow and loss are constant, but if we all had to go through our whole lives carrying them the whole time, we wouldn't be able to stand it. The sadness would paralyze us. So in the end we just pack it into bags and find somewhere to leave it, because people you love never die. Not completely that is. They live in your mind the way they always lived inside you. You keep their light alive. If you remember them well enough, they can still guide you like the shine of long-extinguished stars could guide ships in unfamiliar waters.

However, my grandmother's death is a thing I have never gotten over. I am not suggesting that I wallow in sorrow or let it drag on to the point of being morose all the time. I am just saying it never really goes away. It is like having a pile of rocks dumped in your front yard. Every day you walk out and see those rocks. They are sharp and ugly and heavy. You just learn to live around them the best way you can. Some people plant moss or ivy; some leave it be. Some folks take the rocks one by one, and build a wall. Others make a memorial out of it, a remembrance for someone gone.

I did not cry the day Vada Frye died, because there was nothing but pleasant memories of the love we shared. She was the first person I had ever seen actually die in person during my 22 years of life, and I can still hear the gurgling sound from deep within her to this very day, but it is not painful. It is peaceful. Death is simply the embrace of eternity, and somewhere out there in the ethos our memories float in exaltation of the time we had together.

To lose someone you love is to alter your life forever. You don't get over it, because it is the person you loved. The pain stops, and there are new people, but the gap never closes. How could it?

The night my grandmother died there were no stars, only memories of the stars that had twinkled in our relationship. Yet, how do you deal with the hurt? It is like an eternal but soft rain, the loose girdle of showers of sorrow. As I wrote this homage to her, I even got out the letters we wrote back and forth when I was away in college. Letters that I had not looked at in years, because I assumed it would be too painful. I simply kept them packed away in an old box to gather the dust of time, but there has never been any dust on our love for one another. I asked myself as I gently unfolded the letters if my aging fingers were still nimble enough to play the keys of remembrances that are but echoes on the plains of time. Oh, if I could look upon her weathered face, take her by her wrinkled hand and feel the warmth of her love in person one more time. Yet, I do still feel it, as it is truly with me each and every day, because I carry it in my heart. I carry it in my kindness toward others. The kindness I so lovingly learned from her.

My grandmother had a love which found in me so totally its complement, its goal, its constant lodestar, that the genius of great men, all the genius that might ever have existed from the beginning of the world, would have been less precious to my grandmother than a single one of my defects.

My grandmother was not a philosopher, but she used to say with great conviction that "words have no bones, but they can break bones." She knew what we all should know: a word can cause more pain, more damage than the sharpest knife. As far as she was concerned, saying something and doing something were exactly the same. Still, she saw nothing but good in me, even when I did bad things. For that reason, I tried valiantly to never do anything that might diminish me in her eyes.

Over the years I have grow to realize that death ends a life, not a relationship. I understand that grief and love are conjoined. You do not get one without the other.

I have had two failed marriages, because there must have been something missing in me that drove my wives into the arms of other men. I carry no animosity toward them, because my grandmother taught me darkness cannot drive out darkness: only light can do that. Hate cannot drive out hate, only love can do that.

Perhaps all my life I have been looking for a substitute for my grandmother, trying to find a woman who could live up to the towering example set by her. I believe I have finally found that in my current wife, who comes the closest to being like my grandmother (and my aunt Willa Mae who was my grandmother's daughter) of anyone I have ever met. Goodness cannot be effectively described. It just is.

My grandmother was the exact definition of a good person. A truly good person will speak truth, act with truth and stand for truth. A truly good person is not afraid to think from their heart; therefore, allowing the utter complete crystallization of nonconformist decisions, viewpoints and perspectives to lead their life.

THE DAY VADA FRYE DIED

By following their heart, they stand with their conscience.

It was from my grandmother I learned that the language of light can only be decoded by the heart, and she always had a heart of gold. I realized this all the days I was privileged to share her time on this earth and especially *THE DAY VADA FRYE DIED!*

www.ingramcontent.com/pod-product-compliance
Lightning Source LLC
Chambersburg PA
CBHW060507030426
42337CB00015B/1778